THE GIRLFRIEND EFFECT

HOW TO INCREASE INTIMACY, PASSION AND LOVE BY GIVING YOUR HUSBAND THE GIRFRIEND EXPERIENCE

JODI HARMAN

PUBLISHED BY CHICKLIT

Cover designed by Jodi Harman and ChickLit

Jodi Harman
website at **www.JodiHarman.com**

Printed in the United States of America

First Edition
ChickLit Media

ISBN 978-1-935598-88-6

Table of Contents

Preface: Bring Back That Loving Feeling

G o back to the time when you were dating. You didn't know each other well, yet, but the excitement and giddiness were palpable every time you saw each other. Sometimes, just thinking about him made you happy inside. When dating, you spent hours talking in person or on the phone, you wanted to know everything about each other. As the attraction grew, you began to have feelings for each other. You wanted to spend every waking moment together, and you put your best self forward.

Before every date, you would spend what seemed like endless time preparing. Fixing your hair and makeup, trying on different outfits; you wanted to look your best. You also made sure that you were well-behaved and talked about things that were important, but did not do things that might put yourself in a bad light or cause conflict to arise. Essentially, you hid some part of yourself. Some people may even pretend to like something they do not usually like, just to please the other in this twitterpated, whirlwind romance phase.

As the relationship progressed and you decided to get married, you probably still did not let your guard down. Often, the stress of wedding preparations cause some couples to have disagreements, but they are dismissed as wedding jitters. I actually remember agreeing to watch "The Three Stooges" on our honeymoon because I did not want to disappoint my new hubby, I hated every moment of it (yes, he knows now).

Once the honeymoon was over and you settled into life and responsibilities, oftentimes people become relaxed. Before you know it, what used to not bother you now does because you are with each other more. Living together puts new pressures on you both as you begin a life together. All of a sudden, two individuals that came from different upbringings and circumstances are living together and, sometimes, life throws a curve ball causing contention as you get used to being together.

As children enter the scene, there's new fun and love but also pressure and stress. Women may withdraw from their husbands a little and men feel left out, but neither wants to burden the other with the complaint. However, it's still there and often shows up in the worst way. Instead of addressing this, couples end up fighting and arguing over the little things that the other is not doing or something that is bothering them.

What happened in your marriage to make those wonderful, lustful feelings go away? One of the biggest mistakes that couples make as they start to get comfortable in the relationship is they let the little things bug them. Even worse is when they try to change each other. Both husbands and wives stop trying to make the other person a priority. Somewhere, sometime in the relationship one or both partners have stopped caring as much. As these feelings progress, one or both partners start to wonder why they are in a relationship, especially when they do not feel their needs are being met.

When these feelings arise, one person often starts to withdraw from the other. The problem is that they choose to withhold love and affection until their partner shows it first or makes a change, but the partner may not know how to change or understand the expectations of their spouse. Neither one is willing to take that first step towards healing the relationship.

If you want more love, passion, and positive attention from your spouse, then YOU must show it first.

The Girlfriend Effect will help you ignite that passion and love in your marriage as you focus on making your husband the #1 priority in your life.

This book is the result of my burning desire to know if there is more to life than going to work, cleaning house, and just trying to make it through another day. I was living my life on auto-pilot. I loved my husband, but I felt our marriage lacked something... I knew I needed to make changes, but what?

As I searched for options to resolve my dissatisfaction, I examined every part of my life to discover what would make me happy.

Like every relationship, we had our ups and downs. As I thought about the options to solve my dissatisfied life, divorce entered my mind. Thinking this through, I knew I had a choice to make. I pictured in my mind, someday in the future, seeing pictures of my husband and his new wife with MY children and their new life; or I could erase that future and work to make my marriage better. I had to stop putting all the blame for the wrongs in our marriage on him and own up to what I was not doing to make our relationship better.

I decided to change myself, take charge of how I showed up in life, and to give my husband The Girlfriend Effect experience. I jumped into action learning everything I could about how to be a better wife and lover, a journey that I think will take me a lifetime to finish. I did not know my own potential for sex appeal and how improving my self-confidence would change my life and marriage.

I had to fall in love with me to allow my husband to fully love me. Let's just say, I had some work to do on myself.

The Girlfriend Effect is the journey I created to be the best wife, lover, and version of myself I could be. A journey that I will be on for the rest of my life.

I admit, I have not always been nice to my husband. I have not been the amazing Girlfriend that I could have been, honestly, because I did not know how. Mark and I have gone through some really rough experiences in our relationship. The day I realized I was feeding into those problems was a big wake-up call for me. For so long, I had blamed Mark for everything that was going wrong. I TOOK A BIG LOOK IN THE MIRROR. I was playing the role of victim and felt sorry for myself as if I had no control.

While on my journey to make my relationship better with my husband, I came across a quote from Stephen Covey. It challenged me to be better at loving my husband just the way he was. This statement gave me power to do what needed to be done. Steven Covey listened to a man that stated he did not know what to do because he wanted a divorce. Steven Covey's reply is simple and profound.

"My wife and I just don't have the same feelings for each other we used to have. I guess, I just don't love her anymore and she doesn't love me. What can I do?"

"The feeling isn't there anymore?" I asked.

"That's right," he affirmed. "And we have three children we're really concerned about. What do you suggest?"

"Love her," I replied.

"I told you, the feeling just isn't there anymore."

"Love her."

"You don't understand. The feeling of love just isn't there."

"Then love her. If the feeling isn't there, that's a good reason to love her."

"But how do you love when you don't love?"

"My friend, love is a verb. Love - the feeling - is a fruit of love, the verb. So love her. Serve her. Sacrifice. Listen to her. Empathize. Appreciate. Affirm her. Are you willing to do that?"

-- Stephen R. Covey, The 7 Habits of Highly Effective People: Powerful Lessons in Personal Change

We both chose to have hope and not give up. We made a commitment to make our marriage a priority, no matter what!

I realized I needed to change and become a Girlfriend again! There were times that I have had to stop being selfish, to force myself to be nice, and to put the needs of our relationship, and of Mark, first. I stopped all the drama, fighting, and nagging. I made a conscious decision to bring back fun, excitement, sex, and love back into my marriage. This was the best decision I have ever made. It has made a world of difference in how we treat each other because our relationship is the biggest priority in our lives.

We both put forth the effort because we desire happiness.

When people find out how long we have been married, I always like to add, "We still like and love each other." Loving your husband does not mean the same thing as liking him. These are two different emotions. However, when you like and love someone it makes the relationship complete and happy. If you think about the structure of a building, the "like" is the foundation and bricks that build the frame of the relationship. The "love" and intimacy is what bonds and holds the relationship together – the mortar.

Honestly, you cannot have love without like!

In this book I have outlined simple, tried and true processes that you can implement today to bring love, intimacy, and passion back into your marriage. If you are not already doing some of these things and are worried about being overwhelmed, I would like to introduce the "5% more" rule. I learned this from some of my favorite mentors, Tiffany Peterson and Jack Canfield. Do not feel overwhelmed. Do one thing to be a Girlfriend in the next 48 hours and continually add in 5% more that you are not already doing. You will do 5% more consistently for a whole week, and then each week you add more. Eventually, you will be living with new habits.

Remember, you cannot change your relationship overnight, but you can start small, then add 5%. By the end of 2-3 months you can have the whole Girlfriend experience happening in your life.

However, Some marriages can't be saved. It hurts both parties, but it is important to do what is right for you. You have to decide if life will be better with or without him, then take steps to make your life the best it can be. If you choose to stay together, you both have to be willing to work at the relationship, but one person can make a difference by starting. If you loved each other once, you can bring it back and fall more in love than when you first got married. My husband, Mark Harman, is on this journey with me as we make our marriage a priority and fall madly in love with each other.

Note from Jodi: This book was written with the life of a busy women in mind. The chapters are short and to the point, so you can just pick it up and read wherever you are, not necessarily cover to cover. There may be some places that talk about the same thing on purpose because you really need to pay attention. Just start living the Girlfriend Effect and work your way through the book. You won't regret it.

Jodi Harman

Mark & Jodi Harman

JODI HARMAN

The Girlfriend Experience

JODI HARMAN

Why the Girlfriend Is Needed

*T*he Continental Divide. At times, the trials of everyday life gets in the way. Couples need a way to escape the doldrums and run into each other's arms.

Pretending that you are boyfriend and girlfriend again allows you to focus on the fun and excitement you experienced at the beginning of your relationship. By allowing yourselves to feel carefree, to just be together and enjoy touching, caressing, and being intimate, you can release tension and stress.

I am sure you have had those days, weeks or even months that just take everything out of you. No matter what you do or how hard you try, the trials seem to pile high. Before you know it, you have gone several days, weeks, months without saying a kind thing, kissing, touching or even having sex. The disconnect from your hubby has started and before you know it, there is a continental divide growing between you. Separating you. The whole time you think to yourself... *We need to work on this. We need to spend time together. I miss him. We need to talk. I want to be touched.* Always wondering if your hubby feels the same.

If you are
acting like
his *Girlfriend*
He won't
need to
Look for one

~*Jodi Harman*

You know you want him, but you aren't brave enough to make the first move.

Here's a secret, your hubby is feeling the same way! Most men love and adore their wives. But when life gets in the way it can build up feelings of regret. This is a time when miscommunication and arguments can happen. If this is allowed to continue for long periods of time one of the two, or even both, will feel like giving up. When couples talk about divorce or separation, you know that both husband and wife have not been in the girlfriend and boyfriend roles. These situations can be avoided with a change in mindset: you need to be the girlfriend / boyfriend. Remember you were once in love and had good times together.

If any of this sounds like what is going on in your relationship you need to start acting like The Girlfriend.

I know that relationships take two people. I have designed the Girlfriend Effect as something special that you can do for your relationship with your hubby. From this day forward I want you to commit to change how YOU feel about yourself, your husband, and your relationship. If you commit to just do a few of the things in this book it will make a huge difference.

Yes, I am asking you to change yourself and how you behave. Right now, I want you to focus on what YOU can do to increase love and passion in your marriage.

I am sure that your husband will start to notice some changes in how you act and react. He may be surprised by some of your actions (or non-reactions) as you start to live the Girlfriend Effect and wonder what you are up to. I have created a love letter for you to give him that will explain a little about what you are doing, without telling him everything (some day you can fill him in on the rest).

Log on to our website www.GirlfriendEffect.com to personalize and send your love letter.

Log on to the website

www.GirlfriendEffect.com

to personalize and send your love letter

Girlfriend Mindset

oth husbands and wives want to feel appreciated, loved and closer to each other. One person cannot do it alone, but someone does have to make the first move.

Many women feel that they are the only ones working on their marriage. Women often feel the burden of trying to please their man is too high and give up. Perhaps you feel that HE should be the one making changes. The truth about men is they essentially want the same things as women. In working with many couples, I have found that both husbands and wives crave a better relationship but do not know how to start or even what to do.

The problem with this is that the relationship comes to a halt. Both husband and wife holding their ground. No one is moving forward because of the hurt, anger, regret, frustration, and stress that has built up between them. Once in a while, you may have little triumphs when you are getting along and life seems to be pretty good, but it doesn't last. If you are experiencing this relationship rollercoaster, it's time to get off the ride and do something about it.

The Girlfriend Effect is a frame of mind that drives certain behaviors, and these behaviors strengthen your relationship. You will find that life is made up of many triumphs and good times, and even if there are occasional dips or stress, being the

Girlfriend, you will be able to pull things back to together quickly.

A Girlfriend is full of confidence, friendship, love, intimacy, romance, and, yes, sex. I want you to always have your "Girlfriend Mindset" switched to the on-position. Every time you notice a little hint or a way to improve your relationship, you take note of it. I like to think of it as a minimized window on a computer screen. When the window is open and active in your thoughts, you are thinking about how to create the right atmosphere for your relationship. There may be times when you will need to power down some of the other window screens, the ones that focus on work, being a mom, being a friend, volunteering, and all those other things we do. But the window that focuses on your relationship with your husband should be open at all times. Minimize it if you need to focus on other things, but if it is operating in the background, it is easier to turn it back on in the moment.

Intentionally placing this much focus on how your relationship is working and making mental notes about how to improve it will make all the difference in the world.

Allow me to explain more. Your brain is really smart and sorts information to determine what is important for you to pay attention to at every moment. One of my favorite mentors, Jack Canfield, explains how it works in simple terms.

The human brain has this amazing tool called the reticular activating system. It operates full-time to bring to consciousness the information appropriate to our current intentions. In a sense, the brain learns to ignore repetitive, meaningless stimuli while remaining sensitive to others.

For instance, when you're driving and feeling hungry what do you notice? All those fast-food billboards. If you suddenly realize your gas gauge is on empty, your focus changes to finding a gas station.

When you form inspired intentions linked to powerful emotions, the reticular activating system filters out what you don't need and lets in those resources you do need—the people, ideas, and possibilities. Those resources were there before, but you weren't seeing or sorting them, because you were focused on fast food, gas stations, or something equally mundane. Now, however, you see the valuable resources that match your desires, beliefs and align with your goal. You start to perceive opportunities, attract supportive people, and take actions that accelerate your success.

~ Jack Canfield, Success Principles, 2015

The keywords above are inspired intentions linked to powerful emotions. Love is the most powerful emotion humans feel. As you use the love you have for your husband to intentionally increase intimacy in your marriage, you will be open to ideas and opportunities to improve your relationship. Committing to the Girlfriend Effect will make your relationship the number one priority in your life. Placing yourself in the Girlfriend role allows you space to create new habits. Do not use the excuse that you are too busy. I have worked two full-time jobs, been a full-time student, and a mom with a busy family. We still found time to spend together without other interruptions. We found the time because it was important.

We found the time because our relationship matters.

There are simple actions you can start with that will bring you together after a long day. Make dinner together and talk. Send him a sexy, sideways look that says "I'm thinking of you". Rub his shoulders. Slap his butt. Give him a big hug and press your whole body against his whole body. These things only take a few seconds of your time, but can make a huge deposit into your relationship.

If he needs some silent down time in the evenings, use that to your advantage. Greet him with a real kiss, not just a peck. Let him relax and avoid sharing the little annoyances of the day or nagging him. Instead, flash him a sexy look or body part and see how he reacts. If you are wrestling with kids and dinner after a long day, make eye contact and flirt over dinner. Make it light-hearted and fun for both of you. These little changes only take a few seconds, but could change your relationship forever. Keeping the spark of love alive during these times is vital. The idea is to simply find ways to add some love into what you already do.

Remember, it is about finding one or two things to change, adding 5%, and changing your habits over time.

very sexy   daring

confident   Lovely

self-reliant

affectionate

Sweet poised   carefree

adorable

fearless compassionate

brilliant

audacious   erotic

loving

Girlfriend

exciting   adventurous

gorgeous   intimate comforting

brave   Flirt

cute kind   assertive

valiant   Friend

passionate

gorgeous   sensual

Defining a Girlfriend

As a woman, you have so many amazing qualities and attributes, but I want to focus on a few that define the Girlfriend Experience so you can bring love, passion and intimacy back into your marriage:

Best Friend
Confident and Sexy
Adventurous and Fun

A girlfriend makes sure her man feels loved, appreciated and cared for because he is important. He is a priority. You may feel that you are already exhibiting these attributes, but I need you to understand them as they relate to being a Girlfriend, not just in general.

A Girlfriend is a Best Friend to Her Husband

Most women have a best friend to share everything with and, often, this is another woman. They feel that they need to have a woman to talk to, someone that understands what they are going through in life. Someone to share their deepest secrets and wishes with, someone they trust and look forward to talking with. The important things to ask yourself are: Do you share more of your dreams and wishes with this female friend or with your husband? Do you spend more time with your friends than you do with your husband? Do your friends know secrets that your hubby doesn't? When you have a spare moment in the day, do you think about calling your hubby or your friend?

If you are sharing your feelings with anyone other than your husband, you are leaving him out. This causes a divide in your relationship. I fully understand that some men may not want to hear all about shopping, work stress, or even certain emotional feelings.

But have you ever taken the time to ask your husband if he wants to talk? What does he know about your day to day challenges? Does he know how you feel? Do you call your friends because that is what you are used to doing?

Your best friend should be your husband. Share everything with your hubby. What you would normally talk to your girlfriends about, you should also share with your hubby. Yes, even the girly stuff. If you are withholding parts of your life, how can he fully know you and love you?

This also means that YOU get to talk about what HE likes and doesn't like. What are his interests and hobbies? Fishing, hunting, sports, cars, hobbies...whatever he's into, you should also take an interest. If you are not interested in any of the things he likes, try learning about it and you might like it. For instance, my husband loves basketball. He played in high school and college, now he is a basketball official traveling around the country. This is something he loves. I was not really interested in basketball but as I started attending his games and asking questions, I have come to like it. I will never love it the way that he does, but I love to watch him do something he enjoys.

As you begin to show interest and ask questions, remember this should not feel like an interview or an interrogation. Learn a little bit at a time by spending time with him or do your own research before you start asking questions, this will really impress him and show that you care. When I wanted to learn about basketball, I asked him to take me to a game and explain what was going on. He loved sharing this experience with me, so we continued make this something we did regularly.

You can also take time to learn about each other's careers or businesses. Ask questions and be genuinely interested to know what is going on in his life. Men and women put a lot of time, effort and energy into their careers (this includes parenting). Take the time to share about your career, what you do all day, what you love, and where you want to be in the future.

If this is not something that you have already been doing you may have to ease into it. If you are at a point in your marriage where you are not communicating much you will need to build trust, and love, as this sharing occurs. We will dive into these situations later in the book, for now, just know that as a wife living the Girlfriend Effect you should also be his best friend.

A Girlfriend Always Radiates Self Confidence

*Y*ou are in control of the messages that you send out. I call this the "Confidence Attraction". If you want your husband to notice you more, then you need to become a master of the Confidence Attraction.

The image you project to the world that you are, in fact, confident, in control, composed, and credible will almost demand that people respond to you that way, especially your husband.

Self-confidence and self-esteem are often interchanged but a good mentor of mine, Tiffany Peterson, helped me realize they have slightly different meanings. For instance, you can be self-confident in a specific thing, like a college degree in psychology or math. If you love to cook, research new things, and others love what you make, you are confident in cooking. Confidence means you understand it and can talk about it, even have an entire career based on what you have mastered. Some women are confident in motherhood (or at least stages).

When you look at self-confidence this way, what are you confident in? Are you confident with yourself? Are you confident in your relationship with your husband?

Self-esteem is being confident in your self-worth, abilities, and having respect for yourself, your thoughts, body and feelings. You notice all the amazing things about yourself. You love yourself the way you are. Self-esteem is about loving yourself without judgment and in acknowledgement of all your flaws. Giving yourself the respect and attention you need. Do you take care of yourself? Do you make yourself a priority?

Self-confidence: confidence in ones' abilities and power. A feeling of trust in ones' qualities and judgment. Being secure in yourself and your abilities.

Self-esteem: Having respect for yourself and your abilities. Confident in ones' own worth. Valuing yourself.

All too often, women only notice their flaws, the things they do not know how to do, and how they compare to others. Some think that because they have never had self-confidence or high self-esteem, they will never be able to get it. But let me assure you, both can be learned with practice and a little attitude change when examining yourself and your abilities.

Many women have the mistaken idea that because they do not have the perfect body, smile, clothes, or even living conditions that they will not be able to have self-confidence. Perhaps, they even negotiate with themselves in their mind, "When life gets better, I will be happy and have more self-confidence." You do not have to have the perfect body, smile, or clothes to be a confident, sexy woman. In reality, how you feel about yourself will tell others how to treat you.

The Girlfriend Effect is all about having both self-confidence and self-esteem, and using them to super charge your relationship with your hubby. You have the power within you to change your

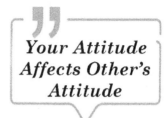

Your Attitude Affects Other's Attitude

relationship and make it better. Your self-confidence brings out your unique beauty more than anything else. Confidence is sexy! When people sense that you are confident in who you are, they want to talk to you and be around you.

Sexiness is built on self-confidence. Look at *Dana Elaine Owens, a.k.a. Queen Latifa.* She is confident in herself and who she is. When you look at her, most do not notice that she is overweight but that she is beautiful and sexy. Self-confidence does not mean bragging to everyone about who you are, or being obnoxious about demanding things. It is knowing that you are powerful in your own right. This is what people will notice when you walk in the room. When you have the right attitude and you are confident in yourself, you are in a position to uplift others. People will naturally be drawn to you and want to spend time with you.

Most importantly, your husband will notice the change in you. When you are confident in yourself, you will be more willing to be open and share yourself with him. He will be drawn to your happiness. This is when the magic happens, you open yourself up to fully loving and caring for your husband and he sees a new, confident, desirable woman. It's a game changer. If you do not feel you have this confidence don't worry, you can get it! Self-esteem and self-confidence are like muscles, they must be worked out and developed in order to show strength. The more you work on, them the better they will be. Confidence and high self-esteem is not something I have always had. I have struggled, just like everyone else. There were times I did not feel like being intimate or having a close relationship with my husband. I realized this was causing a problem in my marriage and I began to work on myself. Once I began to love myself and take care of myself, I had more love to share and to give to my relationship. It changed the way I loved my husband. Both of us have been amazed how these simple daily tips can have a significant impact on the stability of our marriage and the love we have for each other. Now it is your turn. Use the following tips to begin working on those self-esteem and self-confidence muscles. As with any exercise regimen, it takes time to see the results but I guarantee you will be thankful you invested the time and energy to work on your Confidence Attraction.

Work on your Confidence Attraction

1. Radiate confidence by simply altering your body language. This is like a massive energy boost, it will instantly change how you feel about yourself. When you are talking to others, check your posture to make sure you are in an open-body stance with your shoulders back, chin lifted and out front a little. Place your feet about shoulder width apart and lean in a little to conversations. This will make people perceive you as more confident.

If you are listening to someone else talk, slightly lean in toward that person and turn up the edges of your lips (hint: put your tongue on the roof of your mouth it makes your smile look more genuine). To remain calm, cool, and collected, use your hands minimally as you speak. Do not point with one finger, rather, use your entire hand to gently gesture in the direction needed. Just make sure you don't slap someone in the process.

If you are trying to be sexy, it is okay to cross your legs, but this is not ideal if you're in a business setting. Your husband will love your legs crossed if you are flirting and trying to get his attention. Watch yourself in the mirror to see what your face looks like when you talk about different topics. If you are flirting with your husband, then give him a sweet or sultry smile. If you are in public, pay attention to how you look when you smile, get surprised, and how your resting face looks. Make sure that it is always pleasing and approachable. Try not to have a furrowed brow or a grumpy look on your face, as this distracts from confidence.

2. Accept compliments.

Do you know how to accept compliments? If someone compliments your clothes do you deflect by saying, "oh it's nothing". Do you question the person who gave the compliment? Your husband can help boost your confidence more than anyone else. However, if you brush off his kind words, sooner or later he will stop giving them.

Challenge: every time you receive a compliment, I want you to acknowledge the person and say, *thank you*. Then, I want you to internalize the compliment. I want you to really feel it and let it sink into your thoughts and heart. And then say to yourself: *Yes, I do look great today* or *yes, I am smart* (repeat the compliment to re-affirm what was said) repeat it over and over until the little voices in your mind that usually say negative things back are repeating the compliment, too.

I also want you to give yourself some compliments and self-love:

1. Look in the mirror and give yourself a compliment. Something sincere - no sarcasm allowed!
2. Honestly smile at yourself and say thank you back, looking yourself in the eye.

You did ____ so well today.
You were so nice today when ____happened.
You accomplished a lot today- list

This may take some practice. But once you start to accept compliments you will actually get more. Continue to give yourself compliments and love yourself using this exercise every morning and evening. The following Mirror Exercise affirmations, adapted from mentor Tiffany Peterson, will help cement this practice. Feel free to replace with the words/affirmations with what you need to hear.

Mirror Exercise

I love myself and I am enough

I trust myself

My needs are important

I take care of myself

I forgive myself

I am worthy and deserving

I am positive and happy

I am creating the life I want & deserve

I am incredible person

I am beautiful

I am SEXY

Look yourself in the eye and say phrases
with meaning and love to yourself

و. Learn to love your body and yourself.

I had to do this. I had to feel better about myself. I had to accept who I was. I used daily affirmations and a program from my friend, Ann Webb, called "Ideal Life Vision" (ILV) to help. I listen to my Life Vision every day and it helps me be more confident. This is a process I use to improve myself and my attitude. I also create the relationship and life I want.

Ideal Life Vision is all about Minute Clarity, Focus, and Implementation

Minute Clarity: The first requirement to having what you want, is knowing what you want. Most people can give you a detailed list of what they DON'T want; but how many people actually articulate - in minute detail - the things they desire in all areas of their life? Ideal LifeVision is a minutely detailed declaration of intent/personal mission statement that includes the 5 key areas of your life: your relationships (family and social), your spirituality, your physical fitness, your financial/professional life, and your emotional/personal development. Your Life Vision is first created on paper (or computer) in sections. It is fine-tuned and tweaked until it feels complete as an expression of the "ideal you". (Typically runs between 5-10 pages typed! Now that's detail!)

Focus Daily on Your Ideal Life: Your LifeVision is then recorded with specific music and listened to daily. The process of listening daily to the ideal life you intend to create is incredibly powerful. It is a cause in motion that literally activates and attracts the things you desire into your life. The

Ideal LifeVision system puts your "ideal life" on the front burner daily, thus integrating these dreams into your life swiftly and efficiently. By listening to what your "ideal life" looks and feels like daily, you begin taking steps in that direction immediately. Because of the unique recording method, even when daydreaming and not particularly "listening" to your dreams, your subconscious mind still "hears" and responds. Each and every day you are FOCUSING on what you want and the gap narrows between where you currently are and where you want to be. By listening daily to the type of person you are becoming, your beliefs begin to change. These beliefs, which in turn create habits, begin to give way to new beliefs, thus creating new habits. This is literally a tool where you can change your beliefs and actions over a period of time thus reinventing yourself, if you so desire.

Not Another Self-Help Program: As you know, there are hundreds of success and self-help titles lining the bookstore shelves. There's a wealth of knowledge with incredible ideas based on sound principles. And yet most of us are still lacking the results we desire by reading the books. Why? Good ideas are a dime-a-dozen. How to assimilate the ideas, making them a permanent part of our lives, is missing. It's all theory until it's put into practice. Ideal LifeVision is not another self-help program. It's an implementation system; taking your goals and ideas and assisting you in their application. From now on any time you read about or want to act upon a new idea or tackle a monumental goal, you will know exactly HOW to convert or implement it into your life. This tool can be used in overcoming addictions and bad habits as well.

Key Elements:

A word picture of the "ideal you" living your "ideal life".

Includes the motive for wanting to achieve the details of your vision (Your "WHY").

Includes the How, Where, and When (the action plan) of specific goals.

An implementation system for new self-improvement ideas.

Recorded to super-learning music that can put the brain/mind in a meditative state.

To learn more, or create your own Ideal Life Vision, you may check it out at www.jodiharman.com.

Here is a small sample of the relationship part of my ILV:

Ideal Life Vision

Spouse is the center of my life.
I love Spouse so much and he is my best friend
We have fun together.
He is perfect in every way.
He is handsome, clever, stimulating & happy.
I love him unconditionally.
I can talk easily with Spouse about anything,
anytime, always being honest.
We respect each other.
We make our relationship a priority
We spend quality time together every day.
Our intimate life is enjoyable and exciting.

A Girlfriend Is Adventurous and Fun

Living the life of the Girlfriend Effect means you should be having fun with your husband. Many times in marriages, especially as children arrive, couples forget to have fun together. As life gets busy with careers and family you may just be too tired to do one more thing. Think of it like this, you know when you are planning something big like a vacation or a new home or a new job and you get all excited and dream about what life will be like on the vacation or in a new house or at a new job. You find yourself fantasizing about your new life, wishing it would come sooner. Just the thought of it brightens every moment and allows you to get through one more day because there is something to look forward to. This is how you should feel living the Girlfriend Effect, spending time with your man should be the highlight to each day.

When was the last time you laughed together? Is life too serious? Do you feel that you have too many responsibilities to take time away? When was the last time you went on a date? When was your last couple's vacation, have you even been on a vacation alone since your honeymoon? Do you take time to run away on the weekends?

Having fun, laughing and playing changes the chemical makeup in your brain and body. It heightens feelings of love toward your partner and makes you feel happier. This is why it is so important to spend time together and share experiences with your husband.

I know many people that take vacations without their spouse. Like a girlfriend's getaway or a guy's adventure weekend trip. These are fine as long as you are also doing something together, just as often. But, what if you do not like what your spouse likes?

There are two ways to look at this:

1. Find new adventures you can both enjoy. Take some time to figure out a new hobby or interest by trying a few things out. You might be surprised at what is fun when you do it together.

2. Take turns going on the adventure the other person likes. For instance, I do not like surfing in big waves, but my husband does. I will go be supportive. I'm his photographer and cheerleader as he pursues his fun. This goes the other way, too. For instance, I like to look at antiques, my husband is not fond of shopping. Since we decided to do this together, he has found he does like it because it gives us a chance to talk and share memories from when we were young.

One idea for adventures you can enjoy together, is to be creative in the bedroom. Most men say they want more adventure in the bedroom. If you are closed to this suggestion, I ask you to reconsider your feelings on this and keep an open mind as you go through this book. Whether you need to improve your self-esteem and self-confidence in order to feel sexy, or if you need to build trust in your husband and feel closer to him before this can take place, I encourage you to be open to the possibilities. Your willingness to be adventurous and experiment in your intimate life will also become more enjoyable as you live the Girlfriend Effect. Read the chapters on Flirting and Foreplay to spice up your romance and add adventure to your relationship.

Some may think this is compromise, and that is true, but as you take turns enjoying and sharing moments you will become closer. Often people are not happy in life because they are looking for others to create happiness for them. Living the Girlfriend Effect can bring a new perspective to how you feel about yourself and your husband. You can create the happiness you want and allow love to deepen as you share your life together.

Checking Back Into Your Marriage

*a*s you are reading this, you may be wondering what you have gotten yourself into. This sounds like a lot of work, especially if you are the only one working on your relationship right now.

The old saying "a marriage takes two people to make it work" is partially correct. One of you has to make the first move. I believe that living the Girlfriend Effect will create new habits that will lead to meaningful changes in your relationship, changes that will increase intimacy, passion, and love. If this is what you want, YOU have to start to create it.

Creating a fulfilling and loving marriage does take work, especially if you need new habits to rebuild or enhance what is missing. Once you start, I promise your husband will start to pitch in and help with the romance.

The key to making the relationship work is to work on your personal attitude and perception of things. With simple little changes you will see results.

Creating new habits is crucial to growth and fulfillment in a marriage. There are probably some habits you are doing right now that prevent your relationship from growing and may be causing some bad attitudes. Habits are developed by doing the same thing over and over again. You may be so used to doing these things that you do not know it is a problem, it's just what you do.

> **Check back into your Marriage**

When people refer to "living life on autopilot" it means their life has become so routine that it requires little thought process to function. Life becomes a mundane practice of making the same choices day in and day out. Now if this describes your marriage relationship, you can understand why affairs happen and why relationships get boring. It is because of the bad habits. Life on "auto-pilot" is not fun.

As YOU make changes and improvements, you will begin to feel the love come back and your spouse will (usually) develop new habits as well. Putting an end to the mundane does not require effort from both of you, although it does help if both partners are willing to try. YOU need to examine your behaviors and decide where improvement is necessary, then create new habits to fill any voids.

In a relationship where spouses are pointing fingers at each other, you need to examine the individual issues in order to get to the root of the behavior. Do not re-hash all the old arguments, just look close enough to find the pattern or the behavior that is not ideal. Then you can decide how you will create a new habit for the next time this comes up, using the Girlfriend Effect as a guide.

Creating new habits of romance, intimacy, and love is possible. You need to make your marriage a priority and honestly strive to give yourself, your relationship, and your hubby the love and attention you all deserve. Even if your marriage is strong and going smoothly, there may still be room for growth. If you find yourself in some mundane circumstances and your love-life needs some spice let me recommend a couple simple new habits to implement today.

1. Create a distraction free time before going to bed. This means no TV, cell phones, or computers. Use this time to reconnect and communicate about your day and how much you missed each other. Use this time to talk about your relationship and openly discuss your dreams and desires. Limit how much you talk about others or life circumstances. Do whatever you can to give him quality time and commit to just listening and being present with each other. Make sure there are no other distractions and be a good listener, taking turns talking will help. Women seem to have a hard time of focusing on just one thing. This inability to turn off life's daily grind may inhibit the closeness you desire from your husband.

2. Go to bed at the same time as your husband, if possible. This helps to facilitate the conversations and helps both partners get "in the mood" since intimacy is more likely to happen. Take this time to cuddle, touch and caress each other. Touch is a powerful tool that can lighten stress, help you sleep better, and draw you closer to each other.

If this seems like a huge leap for your marriage right now because you are not talking much or even touching, do not get discouraged. Implementing little changes over time can make a huge impact.

Disconnect and Divorce: The Most Harmful Words in a Marriage

*E*very couple goes through different phases in life where one or both partners may not be happy. Maybe you are even rethinking your choice of getting married. Have you talked about the "D" word, Divorce?

If these thoughts have entered your mind, you are missing an emotional connection. Your emotional needs are not being met, and I can usually guarantee that your husband feels the same way. If your emotional needs are not being met, living the Girlfriend Effect may be tough at first. But before you decide to sign the divorce papers, I encourage you to try it.

The reality of emotional neglect and divorce usually starts small, by keeping score and blaming others. The roles between husband and wife have changed a lot over the last few decades. I think both men and women are running so fast just trying to figure life out, that they end up empty, feeling alone, and under-appreciated, with no energy left to work on the relationship. Both men and women find fault with each other as they try to fit into the roles that the world dictates they need to be in.

If we are keeping score:

Women must be a wife, mother, and career woman. They feel worn out and stressed and plead for help. Women work all day and still have the majority of responsibility for the home and children. They struggle to juggle the needs of everyone in their life, and keep everyone happy. As a result, there's little energy or emotions left to give by the end of the day.

All the while, the pressures on men have become exorbitant, as well. Not only are men still expected to provide for the family financially, but they are also now expected to help at home, help with children, and be a romantic husband.

Both husband and wife end up fighting with each other and just going through the motions of family life. If this sounds familiar, the problem is emotional disconnect which, if left to go on for too long, leads to emotional neglect.

I often hear my female clients complain, "He only wants sex, otherwise he ignores me." "He doesn't listen to me." "He doesn't care about me because he never asks how I am feeling."

Meanwhile the men are saying, "She doesn't care that I work so hard." "We don't have sex enough." "She only wants me home to do chores then complains when I try to help."

Both husband and wife are left feeling disappointed in themselves and each other, with neither willing to talk about it because that hasn't worked in the past. This battle usually goes on for quite some time before one or the other decides to quit. The battle of looking at each other's faults leaves both emotionally dead.

Neglect is one of the biggest problems facing couples. The wife neglects the husband because he does not fit into her idea of a perfect man, as he did when they were first married. Husbands feel neglected as the wife complains, demands more, and gives all her love and attention to children. Both are unhappy and perhaps living as roommates instead of lovers.

Women often feel that their husband is responsible for their happiness and then blame HIM for not making it so. Couples need to understand that each person is responsible for their personal happiness. No one can affect your happiness unless you let them.

You decide if you are going to let outside influences affect how you respond and choose whether or not you will be happy.

You have the power to decide if you will wake up on the right side of the bed and be happy.

You have a choice about how you will react to life, situations, or people.

When trouble is brewing, I frequently see three reactions:

1. *Silence*
2. *Lashing out*
3. *Avoidance*

Silence is a form of communication. What you are not saying speaks loudly and can kill the relationship. A person who lashes out usually ends up saying hurtful things toward, or about, their spouse. The person who avoids everything lives a life of numbness.

Often, facial expressions and body language are on display no matter how you react. Negative reactions shut down all forms of future communication and nothing is ever resolved. Both husband and wife are left with unmet emotional needs and an unhappy marriage.

I must admit, I have been there. I searched and wished for so long that there was some advice that really worked, but never found anything. I had to discover it myself.

Mark, my husband, and I have had our share of trials, some not so bad and others that brought us to the verge of divorce. It wasn't until I took a good long look in the mirror that I realized I was part of the problem, not just my husband. You see the analogies you just read were some of my own experiences, the bickering, resentment, anger, frustration, we have felt it all. And yet Mark and I love each other more now than when we got married. It is a different kind of love, one that is much deeper and more fulfilling.

My story

I was the wife that got to stay home when my children were younger. Mark owned his own business and so, every once in a while, I would help with the business. If money was tight, I did daycare and small jobs for others to help bring in money. Our house was busy with four kids and we always had extra kids over to play. I wanted to be the best mom in the world. I cooked, cleaned, took care of kids, we were a typical family "trying to keep up with the Jones" meaning we had nice cars, a nice big house, and went on vacation all the time.

We thought we were living the dream.

Don't get me wrong it was wonderful and we have so many great memories. I loved our life then and still today would not change a thing - except my attitude!

Yes, my attitude! My husband worked long hours running the family construction business and when he got home, I wanted help. I needed a break. I often had a "Honey Do List" and, yes, I got frustrated that things weren't done. Over the course of about eight months, I started to just do them myself. The problem wasn't that I was learning new skills and being self-reliant (which, I agree, women need to be) the problem was that I was blaming my husband for not being available to help me, even though I could do it myself. I felt unloved and an emotional wall was being built up.

He didn't even know this was happening. He thought everything was okay since I had it all taken care of.

The problem was me! I remember one day getting a babysitter to watch the kids and taking some time to myself. I ended up meditating and praying to figure out how to love my husband so he would love me more. As I was meditating I got a glimpse of what I had been doing to my marriage, my husband. It was as if I was watching a movie. I judged my husband for not helping. I realized that sometimes I did not even ask him to help me, but still got mad because he didn't. When I got upset with him, I would play the victim. As I played the scenes over in my head, I could not believe the way I behaved. I realized that he really did not know what I wanted or needed from him because I did not tell him. Sometimes, my lack of communication meant he did not even know I was upset.

I knew I did not want a divorce, even though I had thought about it before. I really loved him and knew there had to be a better answer.

As I analyzed my own actions, I knew I needed to change in order to save my marriage. I needed to help my husband understand how I felt and that I really did need him and love him. Yes, he needed to make changes as well, but I knew if I changed how I acted toward him, things would change, they would get better. His reactions to me would change if I approached him differently.

Thus, this idea of the Girlfriend Effect took root. I wish I had a book like this that would have helped me understand what we were doing wrong and how to fix it. At the time, I was reading and listening to everything I could get my eyes on to try to change my husband and fix my marriage. But the problem wasn't him, it was me!

As troubles come up and couples are not getting along, they may disconnect, stop sharing, stop talking all together. This is when they really need to be using intimate conversations, a technique I will cover in another chapter. Like me, many couples take the easy way out and choose silence because communication is hard work.

When couples stop talking it causes bigger problems. Besides the silence and fighting that happens, the result is that neither partner feels cared for. There is no place for care, concern or empathy for the other person. This lack of empathy destroys any deeper feelings you had for each other, causing each person to be inconsiderate of the other's needs. Many times they are at an impasse, neither willing to give without the other also giving in return. They start keeping track of who has done what, where and for whom. They also begin not to care for each other and start spending time with other people or withdrawing from the relationship.

When couples show disrespect, selfishness, and resentment toward each other, it starts a tailspin problem that must be fixed if they are going to stay married. You can redirect your relationship and help it get to the next level or at least to the point where both are willing to speak to each other and listen to each other.

In order for the impasse to be corrected and for love and caring to reenter the marriage, the husband or wife needs to step-up and challenge what is happening in the relationship.

Women, take this challenge! You have the power to change how you feel and behave. Use this power to help your husband fall in love with you again. If you are not able to have deep conversations about your hopes and dreams yet, start with talking about little things and spend time together. Put in the effort every day and you will see improvement.

The Girlfriend
Challenge

JODI HARMAN

Banishing Bitchiness

JUST STOP IT!

 $\mathcal{M}$ any women take pride in being bitchy! This is not appealing at all and is a turn-off for most men.

Many women have become obsessed with themselves and do not think about how their mood affects their man's whole world. Ladies, men should not have to walk on eggshells around you! The fastest way to drive your husband away is to be mean, cross, temperamental, and bitchy.

Take a moment to observe when you see a man and woman together in public and the woman is acting like a bitch. Watch the man, he physically moves away or leans, tries to ignore her, and looks broken down. Some men respond with bitchiness of their own because of the meanness delivered toward them, usually men walk away frustrated and shut down.

It is difficult to have tender thoughts or feelings about someone that is mean, unkind, or bitchy. The natural response to that behavior is revulsion. If someone is treated this way, it will often cause the offended person to avoid the circumstances and conversations, thus halting any closeness and loving feelings.

Stop him with a kiss! instead of sharp words

Banish Bitchiness

@Jodiharman
@TheGirlfriendEffect

There is way to get your message across without being bitchy to your man. Decide before you speak how it may affect others around you, especially your husband. Changing your approach, your wording, your attitude, and the look on your face will help change the situation. If you cannot do these things, then you should not say anything. You need to take a TIME OUT!

I admit to acting a little bitchy a few times and I have always regretted it after. I like to think things through before I say them, to make sure they are okay, but even then sometimes men interpret things differently than women. YES, I have hurt my hubby in the past, and I am sure there may be many more times because I am human, but they are few and far between.

It seems that some women use the excuse of PMS to be mean and believe that it somehow makes their behavior okay. I understand, more than you know, what it is like to have hormones out of balance. But that is not a reason to hate the world and be mean to the man you love. It is definitely not an excuse for me to be bitchy all the time. My lack of control over my emotions should not make anyone, especially my man, feel bad or hurt in any way.

You need to check your attitude and look at the reasons behind the bitchiness. Sometimes we have more control than we realize. There was a time when I was mad at the whole world and I blamed everyone else for my bad mood. I stayed in this bad mood for several months, it was just something I could not get rid of. I was mean to everyone. I am not a boisterous person and tend to keep things bottled up more than others. I was using the silent treatment and it was NOT

GOOD. I blamed everyone else for what was going on around me.

One evening, after a very long day, I just wanted to be left alone. My sleep was very restless that night. When I woke up (still grumpy), I went on a long walk hoping my mood would improve before I had to get kids off to school. As I was meditating, I had a very strong thought that all my moodiness and bitchiness was my own fault, that I was the problem – not my husband or kids. I sat there arguing with myself in my mind. This could not be the case; it was not me.

Then I replayed all the events from the past several weeks and I could see myself blowing up over little things and making a big deal over things that were of little concern. I realized IT WAS MY FAULT! I was the one looking for faults in others, especially my husband. I had a good cry and gathered myself together as I went home to apologize for my grumpiness and meanness. I was way out of line. I had put all of my energy into looking for faults and things that he was doing wrong. That day I decided I would start to notice all the good things he does and how he loves me, and my heart was softened once again.

I also realized I had neglected my body. I had missed some vitamins and my food choices were not that great. Occasionally, I did not eat and that caused my blood sugar to tumble and my grumpy self to emerge. I have to admit I am not proud of that time, but it did teach me not to judge and blame others. I have to look at myself and my behavior first.

Several years later I experienced some of the same feelings of anger and maybe a little depression. I knew this time that something was not right with my body, so I made a doctor's appointment. The results showed that my body was not producing the hormones I needed to survive. I was able to get my hormones back within normal ranges over the next month and the symptoms vanished, as did my bitchiness.

Women go through different phases in life... child bearing, menopause, PMS, etc. and you have many hormone changes that will occur. These phases can be severe for some women, but this is not a reason to be mean. If you are struggling with this problem, check with your doctor or a naturopathic practitioner to find out what is going on. If you cannot control your mood changes then please get some help! I am grateful for a doctor that listened to my symptoms and helped me get to the root of the problem.

I am not making any medical claims here, just suggesting that you take care of yourself so that your relationship can be happy and whole.

JODI HARMAN

No More Hubby Bashing

know too many wives who put their husband in the 'dog house'. Ladies, treat your husband like a man and talk to him like an adult.

If you are not agreeing on certain things, sometimes HE is not the problem. I had a friend that one day decided it would be okay to massacre her husband in front of our group of friends. She blatantly threw all her complaints in his face, mentioning all his flaws and her absolute displeasure in him. The whole group stared in embarrassment. I felt so badly for him. Perhaps I do not know the 'behind the scenes' part of the story. But even if I did know, there was no reason a show of emotion like that would have been acceptable. This poor man got up and walked away from the area with his head down.

It is difficult to have tender thoughts or feelings about someone that is mean, unkind, or bitchy. The next time I saw my friend, I decided to ask her what her husband had done that was so horrible that she thought embarrassing him in public was a good idea. I thought perhaps she needed someone to talk to. Her reply to me was, "It's not just one thing he does, but everything he does that bugs the **** out of me. If I have the opportunity to yell at him in public, it feels like I just got him back for bugging me." I then asked her if he abused her or neglected her, she replied NO. She had no other explanation for her outburst except that it made her feel better. I do not ever remember the husband ever fighting back or saying anything negative about his wife.

You have a special power within you to 'make or break' your husband by the way that you speak to him or treat him! There is no way that I would ever treat my husband in that manner, and he would not treat me that way. After witnessing this tragic event I vowed that I would always make sure to be kind to my husband both in public and private. I have since witnessed similar cringe-worthy outbursts and try to offer words of wisdom to the offender, as well as sympathy for the victim. This also brought new light to another instance when husbands are the victims.

NO more
Hubby Bashing!

Early in our marriage my husband and I committed to keeping our private information private, whether it was good, bad or ugly. It has made a big difference in our ability to trust each other. This commitment was made after I came home from being with girlfriends who spent the entire evening complaining about their husbands. The complaints were about the demands of too much sex, husbands not helping around the house, not helping with the kids, or working too much. Now, I am not saying that I did not have some of those same complaints, but I felt so bad for the husbands. I knew their bad habits and some personal information about their intimate life. I just listened without saying anything. I knew how hard my husband worked and that he was tired when he got home. But he always showed me, and told me, that he loved me, so I did not think complaining about him was something I should do. I was very uncomfortable with the conversations. That's when I knew I had a better relationship than the other women in the room.

When I went home I talked to Mark about it and he was thankful for my response. We both felt that it was important that we never talk about each other with anyone else. I did not want my friends to judge my husband wrongly for something I said out of gossip, girl talk, anger, or hurt. We decided to keep private things private.

There were times in our lives that we did not see things the same way or that we disagreed with each other. But we did not take this opportunity to put each other down or say mean things. Rather, we would agree to discuss it after we both had time to think about our point of view. We did not let this time go on forever, usually these discussions happened the same day. We would find time away from everyone else and discuss the problem, each taking a turn to share their own opinion. Most often this 'break for reflection' allowed us to calm down and figure out what was really going on. Looking at a problem from another person's perspective can change how you feel about a problem, often making it not a problem at all. Many times this is a misunderstanding of expectations that one of us had about a situation or incident. We found a way to help each other through the problems together.

If there are times in your marriage that you feel the need to reach out to a friend or confident outside of your relationship make sure this is an exception and not a common occurrence.

It is vital to your relationship that this friend can be trusted to keep things private. Remember that you should use this time to try to talk through a situation and not as a time to belittle, demean or verbally abuse your husband.

Women often find comfort in talking with other women, but remember that your devotion to your marriage should come before the other friendships.

I see this type of behavior displayed in public often and on television constantly. Hollywood has almost made hubby bashing a popular behavior. In many reality TV shows this is the drama part of the show, I am not sure if it is made more dramatic than it is in real life, but considering I have seen it firsthand, I am sure it is real.

I have many concerns about this horrific display of bad behavior.

1. How in the world are children supposed to grow up to respect their parents, especially the father, when their mother constantly airs his faults and wrongdoings? This happens a lot in divorce, but can also be common when couples are struggling. Remember, you are still talking about your child's father. For that matter, I do not think children will respect their mother for talking this way either. She might even be talking to her kids this way. If this is you, please get some help so that you do not drive away everyone that loves you.

2. Words cannot be taken back; they can only be forgiven. Unfortunately, words will always be remembered. If you choose to treat your husband this way, I am positive he is building up walls and resentment toward every word you utter. Please do not do this!

3. A man that is treated in this manner will not want to be the kind and caring husband you wish for, even if he was the perfect man before your words cut him down. He will disconnect from the relationship. He may stop offering love and support.

4. As a friend of the family, I now knew all the secrets of all my friends' husbands. From this evening with their wives I learned: those husbands are slobs, they leave clothes everywhere, they want sex too much, don't brush their teeth, have feet that stink, pick their nose, they are not good in bed, are not good fathers, plus so much more. Having all that information in my head, what do you think happens next time I see any of my friends' husbands? I remember all the bad things she told us about him. It made me uncomfortable as I tried not to pass judgment. It's hard knowing and keeping all their secrets, but I would never divulge private information. So, if you are one of my friends from several years ago and you happen to read this book and remember that night, I hope that you and your husband are doing well now. If you are still experiencing the hubby-bashing problem, you need to keep reading.

If you want to be treated with kindness, love and respect then you should never attack, belittle and hurt the man you love.

Taking Care of Yourself

*E*verywhere we look, there are a myriad of articles, items to purchase, and new fads to help you look younger, feel better, and have an amazing body.

The fashion and media industries have defined the perfect woman to have the perfect body, dress a specific way, and even behave a certain way. Every time you look in the mirror you are judging yourself against the standards of the world.

Why does beauty have to be about what is on the outside? Why are we judged for how we look? It was not until I spent some time working on me that I fell in love with myself. Yes, that's right, I fell in love with myself. I finally love the beautiful amazing person that I am. I know that everything that happened in the past does not define me. I did not always have the self-esteem I have now and there are some days that it waivers, but when I follow the suggestions below, I am successful and happy, and you can be, too.

Living the Girlfriend Effect will help you to love yourself and allow your husband to fully love you too.

The world's view of who I should be is not my destiny. I believe I create my destiny and have the power to change how I feel about myself. This will allow my husband to fully love me. You see, if I do not love myself, it prevents my husband from delivering his full devotion and love to me. It took me a long time to believe that when my husband looks at me, he does not see all my imperfections; he sees me as perfect. Mark has always told me he loves me and has always been attracted to me. There is not a day that goes by that he does not give me several compliments. One day, I just started to believe him. All the years of self-doubt and judgment were gone, and I knew my spirit and my body were beautiful, not just because he said it, but because I actually believed it myself.

Being in the mindset of The Girlfriend gives you permission (if you need it) to have the confidence you need to be sexy, outgoing, attractive, seductive, daring, adventurous, fun, and loving for your relationship. I think this is part of what attracts men to women in the first place.

When most men met their future wife, the initial attraction was physical. Men are most likely to be visually stimulated. This is one of the reasons women need to look good all the time. You don't have to look and act like a super model, but take a look in the mirror and at what you choose to wear every day. Maybe it's been a while since you have updated your wardrobe or bought anything new. Do not become comfortable and complacent just because you have caught your man. You should stay in the courtship phase of the relationship that motivated you to look your best.

Many times, you can look back in relationships and realize that when one person stopped caring about themselves, their spouse noticed the changes, too. Instead of becoming complacent and relaxed, try switching it up the opposite way. I am not saying that there is not a time for jeans and t-shirts, or even sweats. But what I am saying is that you need t ⌐y attention to how you show up for life's events, even the little things. Men and women tend to lose The Girlfriend and Boyfriend experience as comfort overrules the fact that you should be attracting your lover at all times. When you choose to not care enough about yourself that you do not need to get up, get dressed and show up for life, your husband will notice, and the bonds of attraction will begin to loosen.

You need to be able to separate from all the other roles that you may play in your life... mom, caretaker, housekeeper, employee, and the list goes on (more on this later). The idea is to be prepared to always look and act your best with your husband. By physically changing your clothes it allows you to "change" your roles when it is time to be with your husband.

Act as if you are still The Girlfriend! A girlfriend always looks good, smells good and is excited to see her man. Making the extra effort – just 5 minutes to take a look in the mirror, fix your hair and makeup, a quick change of clothes will allow your partner to be attracted to you, just like when you were dating.

Do you feel like a "10" in what you wear? Do your clothes make you feel attractive? Are they out of style? Do they fit correctly? Go through your closet and dresser, get rid of the clothes that do not make you feel like a 10. If you find that you need new clothes, make a list of what you need and purchase when you can. There are several stores that offer personal shoppers to help you mix and match outfits to optimize what you purchase; this is an excellent way to get what you need while saving a little money. Plus, it makes shopping fun. This is not an excuse to go shopping right now, especially if money is tight. Refer to your list when you do shop so you can feel good about what you wear.

What do you wear to bed? Recently I did a survey of over 300 people on social media and asked the same question. The response did not surprise me, 76% responded with: old t-shirt or camisole with old loose-fitting pants or old shorts. I am not bashing the idea of comfort when sleeping but I do want you to notice how you are showing up to spend some time with your loved one. Most often, this is the most valuable time that you have with your husband and far too many women are showing up in raggedy t-shirts and holey pants... Completely unattractive! A woman should make it a point to show up for bed ready and prepared to have an amazing time talking, holding each other, and having sex with her husband. Showing up in raggedy, comfy clothes is not a turn-on and should be avoided.

Take a little extra time when getting ready for bed (the time you will be close) with your husband. Brush your teeth and hair, shave your legs, take care of personal hygiene, and show up in clothes that are attractive, sexy, and say "I want to spend time with you". Now if you are one of those women who say, "I'm not in the mood," that may be because of the clothes you choose to wear. If you do not feel like a "10" in it, you should not wear it. Showing up naked would be better.

When you do not prepare to go to bed together, the idea of intimacy does not happen as often as it should. I actually know women who do not shave their legs as an excuse not to have sex. As a couple you need to fight to keep your relationship alive and happy. Couples who have sex are happier and closer together. Just because you are married, you do not have an excuse to not take care of yourself.

Whether you work, stay home with family or work from home. Show up looking your best every day, in every situation. Do not always look and dress like a mom, just because you are one. If you stay at home most days, get dressed, do your hair and makeup. It does not have to take an hour but just put some effort into how you look. An added benefit with be increased productivity with your work or family responsibilities. This will go a long way to helping you feel confident in everyday life.

JODI HARMAN

Getting Rid of Your Baggage So You Can Be the GIRLFRIEND

*W*arning- this chapter is not sexy or fun, but it is very necessary. This chapter is dedicated to all women who have felt unloved or abused in their lives.

I personally have gone through some really hard things in my life and I am telling you right now, if you allow those memories to hold you back from love and fully enjoying your life then you will always stay where you are and will never experience fulfillment in love and relationships. Allowing the memories of your past to haunt you is not helping you at all.

I am not saying it is easy, I am saying it is worth it.

It took me a long time to get over my issues, and I am sure this is resonating with some of you. After coming through the pain and suffering, I was able to have a loving relationship with my husband.

I know so many women who have a past that is not shareable, but they need to work through it and leave it in the past. I wanted to share with you a few things that may help the process of moving on from a past that was painful. I hope you can learn to use that pain to make yourself stronger.

I think what helped me work through the tough times was that I knew I wanted to have a better relationship with my husband and I wanted to enjoy the intimate time we spent together. I had to acknowledge that if I did not heal from the past, there would be no joy or excitement in the future.

I have experienced growth from each of the items listed below and have made some really great friends along the way. My hope is that you use what works for you and, most importantly, that you get the help you need to enjoy life and your relationship with your husband.

Find the support you need

Husband: Your number one supporter should be your husband. This may be hard for some women, but he loves you and will be more understanding than you ever thought possible. You need to start with opening yourself up to letting him love you and accept the support that he offers. Often women suffer in silence out of shame and embarrassment from past trauma. Once you actually work up the courage to share your feelings, it makes everything better. Plus, when you allow your husband to love you through the rough stuff he will become the trusted advisor and friend that you need for comfort, safety, and love.

Friends: Find friends who can love and support you as well. Sometimes it can be hard to find trust and friendship, especially if you have been hurt in the past. But having a friend you can call to share secrets with and just be yourself with makes life easier.

Get psychological help if needed: Do not be afraid to ask for help if you need it. Ask for a referral from friends and interview several therapists to find the one that you feel comfortable sharing with. There are a lot of new medications that can help, too, so keep an open mind about seeking professional help.

Start a diary or journal: This may be hard as many who have gone through hard things do not want the possibility of anyone else finding their writings. I understand, but I want you to know that writing is really good therapy. If you are worried about others finding what you write, I suggest you write it then have a little ceremony as you destroy it by shredding or burning it. The ceremony helps you to release the pain captured on the page, so I encourage you to try it.

Other ways to move on: My friend, Christi Diamond from www.thehealingcoach.com, knows that pain is a barrier that keeps us from having deep, connected, authentic and meaningful relationships. She helped me understand that healing doesn't have to be so hard and difficult, consuming, or draining.

Forgiveness of self and others is the key to moving forward in lasting and meaningful relationships. By overcoming pain from the past, I was able to step into a place of empowerment. Christi has written a couple of books, *Aroma Heal and Aroma Heal II,* and offers services through her website if you want to learn more.

If your marriage is suffering (maybe you are not even sleeping or having sex with each other), start with little things from this book, and continue to add in more joy and excitement. You will need to take action in some way to communicate that you are trying to work on the relationship and want to make it better.

Discover what is holding you back and be sensitive to the fact that your husband may have issues in his past that are holding him back, too. If one partner has difficulty enjoying intimacy or sex because of events from the past, giving love and support is imperative. Many times, these events can affect communication and our willingness to be open. It may be as if part of them is hiding. Get help to get over the problem so your relationship can flourish. This may take some time and both partners need to be supportive and patient during this time. But trust me, the sooner you get through this the better.

When you are in a Boyfriend and Girlfriend role you will do whatever you can to keep the other person interested and involved in the relationship. You need to be willing to put yourself out there a little bit more, and you need to trust each other. Even though there may have been tough things in your past, do not let the past keep you from achieving the love you desire and need. If you are not ready to share or talk about it, that's ok for now but you need to be able to communicate that with your spouse, so he does not think the he is the problem. Just let him know it is something you are working on and to be patient with you. You will be surprised how supportive and kind the response will be.

Build the Foundation

Giving Love and Attention

*A*sk yourself, 'Why do I want to be a Girlfriend?'

Most women will say they love the attention and affection it provides and fills the necessary innate desires that every person has. Men need and desire the same things, but in different levels. Men love to be touched, hugged, kissed and caressed; they crave it. Guys need to feel loved to be successful in career, life and family.

The idea of The Girlfriend Effect is to make your relationship a priority and give your man the attention he needs and putting his needs first by providing an exciting and passionate relationship.

In the role of a Girlfriend, this means that all your attention is aimed toward your guy. You do things that show your man that you are thinking of him when you are apart. A Girlfriend does cute little things that get his attention. Usually, wives will not do this anymore. Girlfriends that look forward to seeing their man will have a better relationship. Girlfriends do not mind putting the required work into making their guy the #1 priority in their lives. Let's add to the original list of qualities

> *Men love to be hugged, kissed and caressed. They **crave** it!*

and attributes of a Girlfriend to strive for to ignite the spark – lighthearted, playful, not too serious, fun, exciting, sexy, in control of emotions, accepting of herself and others, easy going, fantastic lover, adventurous, daring, etc.

Allow me to share a personal incident that really awakened me to what I was doing to my relationship. When our family was young there were so many days that I longed for peace and quiet and time to myself. There were times when I was waiting for Mark to get home from work just so he could relieve me from my mom duties. Little did I know he sensed that and in return was a little resentful. Of course, having a family is hard on occasion, but I did not look forward to seeing him for the man I was in love with or attracted to, but only as a relief person. One day while handing off the kids for a short break when he got home it finally clicked in my brain; oh my goodness I had neglected him! The man I loved was feeling isolated from me and felt that I did not need him, except to help care for the children. I let my family responsibilities interfere with my relationship with the one man that meant the world to me. Word of advice, do whatever it takes to let your spouse know you love him. As soon as he walks in the door be ready to greet him with a hug, kiss and a happy hello even if your day was not great. Remember, he was away from you all day and probably missed you. Do not ignore him or turn away from the affection he needs and desires.

After some time, my husband noticed I was not doing it so much anymore. So, I told him what I had discovered. He shared with me that he was actually jealous of the kids, especially the babies sometimes. I spent so much of my time with the children that he was often left with the leftovers of my love and affection, honestly, he didn't get much. By the time I got the kids settled in bed and had a moment's peace I felt I had nothing left to give him. Being a mother is wonderful and demanding, but it should not be placed before your relationship with your husband. Yes, children demand a lot of time and attention, but do not just give your husband the leftovers.

Moving forward, I made it a point to pause when we greeted or said goodbye with a hug and a kiss. I made sure to make time for him each evening BEFORE I was exhausted, even if that meant the kids got to watch a little more TV. We both needed to feel loved and connected to each other after being apart all day. Sometimes it was sitting on the couch together. While the kids played, we talked and held each other. It wasn't private time but we did get in some touching and talking.

We have also found that we need to limit the amount of time we use electronics and cell phones. Sometimes, you may be in the same room and kind of having a conversation, but if you are constantly looking at your phones or computers you are not paying attention to each other. Giving your spouse your undivided attention will say I love you more than words.

Here is another idea to get you started living the Girlfriend Effect. See if this sounds familiar, you are both working, after a long day you may need to figure out a time for both of you to decompress. Do not allow the stress of life and kids destroy the love in your relationship. Make sure to schedule time if needed. You may even need to set reminders in your phone to give a kiss or hug or even a sexy look. If you need to set a timer to get started then go ahead, it will eventually become a habit and you will no longer need the reminders.

I actually remember a coworker making fun of me for having a reminder on my phone to flirt with Mark. I was working in a busy hospital and had left my phone on the desk when a coworker saw the notification that popped up. I was only embarrassed for a moment when I realized, I was the one in a great relationship and they were not. Soon they began asking me for advice, which is kind of how this whole book idea came about.

Finding ways to say I love you throughout the day will let him know you love him. The next chapters will help you know what to do in order to treat him to the Girlfriend Effect.

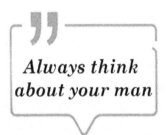

Always think about your man

Now that you have worked on yourself a bit, changed your attitude, and become more mindful of how you are acting and reacting to your husband you can start to embody the Girlfriend he fell in love with. To do that, we are going to start where most relationships start, with a little bit of flirting.

Master the Art of flirting and foreplay... again.

Let's start with just talking to each other first.

If your relationship is suffering from lack of communication, there are a few things I want you to start thinking about. Remember when you first met each other? The excitement you had to just be together and talk? Just thinking of the other person made you want to scream for joy; you were happy. You loved everything about your husband. The way he looked, smelled, walked, talked, and when you kissed, it made you tingle all over and you were filled with passion, love and excitement. The man just swept you off your feet! You were so in love that you never noticed anything wrong with him or if you did, you did not care, because you loved him.

I want you both to get back into that mindset. Start by making a commitment to spend time flirting during the day and communicating in the evenings, and you will be amazed to see those flames reignite.

Staying in contact with your hubby during the day lets him know you are thinking of him and that you miss him. Flirt all the time! Remember when you were young and in love? It felt so nice to have someone compliment and pay attention to you. When couples first start to date they look forward to talking to each other, to being with each other. Send text messages, leave notes, or call to let him know he is on your mind. You can even leave a voice mail if he can't talk.

There is a time and a place to talk about family and home stuff, but that can't be the only thing you talk about. Set time aside each day to discuss how your day was, any problems, kids and family. Use the rest of the day to enrich your relationship and play with each other in your communications. I am pretty sure you are asking yourself how this can be done. Rest assured that when you live the Girlfriend Effect, you find time throughout the day to focus on complimenting your man or getting him turned on while you are away from each other.

If you have something unpleasant to discuss with your husband set a time and place for this to happen when there is no one else around, no distractions, and you both feel safe. Many times, these talks happen in the bedroom because you have privacy. I am going to encourage you to not talk like this in your bedroom. Use a bathroom, closet, another room, or even the car. This keeps your bedroom a place that you can spend time together being intimate and talking about your relationship in positive ways.

For many married couples, the days of flirting disappeared once rings were exchanged. The intimacy and sex should have brought about extra flirting throughout the day and trying to get each other's attention. For some, it may have lasted up to a year after the honeymoon and then dwindled off as couples begin to get comfortable with each other. However, now that sex and intimacy are "not taboo or illegal" the flirting really should have become much more daring and X-rated than ever before. But if it hasn't, all is not lost; you can rekindle the flames. Living the Girlfriend Effect can help bring back the feelings you once had.

Turning it on; flirting and foreplay

Let's talk about it all: the look, the hair, the clothes, dressing sexy, showing a little skin, kissing, flirting, holding hands.

To spice things up now that you share a home, try to create a little mystery before he sees you for date night or intimacy. Getting dressed in another room and not allowing him to see you will help bring back the feeling of when you were dating.

Or better yet, meet at the club or for dinner reservations as if you hadn't seen each other for a while. Hint: make sure to wear lingerie underneath your clothes or, better yet, don't wear any underwear at all. It's a real turn on for guys.

Make him think about you and lust after you all the time! Just the anticipation of flirting, foreplay and sex makes the desire and arousal more intense. Leave little notes with a bright red lipstick kiss on it (your kiss). Give him love notes, text messages all day. Send him a sexy picture of yourself during the day. Have a couple of ideas in your mind of what you want to do to him and be prepared to set the mood until you can rendezvous.

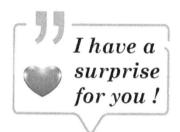

I have a surprise for you !

A text, email, or call saying, 'I have a surprise for you tonight,' is a great way to start. If it's a night in watch a movie, make out, and let your hands go roaming. Or better yet, get a local hotel for the night and surprise him with drinks, dessert, and sex. Give him a night he won't forget.

Make sure to hug and kiss him frequently, especially with skin-on-skin contact. Hold hands and cuddle as much as possible. Rub your hands all over his body paying extra attention to those favorite parts. Take longer to say hello and goodbye with a sensual kiss and body rubbing. Take every opportunity you can to touch him, even a butt-slap tells him you find him sexy.

Tips to Drive Him Wild

Your Look
Men are visual creatures and get stimulated by what they see. Since that is the case, flip on his visual libido switch with a sexy look. Dress sexy when you go out. Something else that is visually stimulating for him is the way you move, stand, and walk. Slow, sensual, exaggerated movements will keep his focus on you. Think about some of those movie scenes you love. How does the woman seduce her man with her moves? Don't always save the sexy dress-up for evening dates. Give him some visual cues on a lunch date or when you go out for drinks with friends. Don't just dress sexy with the clothes he can see, put on sexy lingerie underneath. Give him a quick preview of what is waiting under your clothes and your drinks with friends may end earlier than expected. Keeping him aroused and paying attention to you is the goal. When it comes to lingerie take some hints from him. Pay attention to when he compliments what you are wearing. You will soon know what he likes. Put that knowledge into action by wearing clothes and lingerie he likes. And no, you don't have to dress like a slut. Wear something that makes you feel beautiful and he will love seeing you in it.

Your Voice
Men love their woman's voice so use it. Start with whatever your comfort level is when talking dirty. Saying something sexy when you can't do anything except talk is a great way to connect and share a secret. Describe what you want to do to

him or what you want him to do to you. You don't have to be overly explicit to start, but as you become more comfortable talking to your partner this way, you will open up and Wow! This doesn't always have to be done in person but a sexy phone call or text can start the sexual excitement. Remember it doesn't have to be all at once, just a little at a time. Too much too fast and he may think something else is going on, especially if you haven't done anything like this before. When you do talk dirty to him, note his reactions for future reference and build from there.

Your Lips

Kissing is one of the top ways to flirt and start your foreplay! Not just that little peck but wet, long, lingering kisses. Think teenage make-out session. Everyone likes kissing and we don't do enough of it once we are married. It takes a back seat to 'The Main Event'. There are so many ways to sensually kiss your man. Just start experimenting, watch some great romance movies and copy those hot kissing scenes. Believe me, he will be ecstatic that you are taking the art of kissing to the next level. When you are kissing, imagine it as your only outlet of expressing your love to him and enjoy it.

Your Touch

Something else we seem to forget to do once we are married is to sensually touch each other. We stop holding hands and touching. Do you ever just wrap your arms around him while you are walking? What about those soft brushes of a hand on arm, hand or back? Just a soft lingering touch that says I am here and I am thinking of you. You want your touch to be slow and light, as this will excite his senses.

How you move turns him on

Men are visual creatures, so watching you undress is one of the biggest ways you are able to excite and entice him. When you have his attention and no interruptions, take your time to undress slowly, letting him savor each moment as you seduce him and move into foreplay. Try not to rush things, even though you might feel nervous. Going slow and steady will keep him interested. Think about the romantic bedroom scenes you see in movies. Take your time when removing each piece of clothing. Slowly raise your dress or skirt from the bottom reveling your legs, then thighs. Use your own hands to rub all over your body as if they were his hands, making him wish it were his hands, as if you were massaging your body, legs, sides, stomach and butt. If you have pants on, unzip and unbutton teasingly then pull them down slowly and give a little wiggle as they fall to the floor. As you take off your blouse, unbutton it slowly teasing him and look right into his eyes. If you pull off your blouse flip your hair and give him a side-view sultry smile as it flies off. Finally, you are down to what he has been waiting to see, your lingerie. Do a couple seductive dance moves so he can fully see how gorgeous you are. As you undo your bra let the straps fall off your shoulders as you cup your breasts with your hands, then drop your bra on the floor. Now that you have his complete attention let him know he will be removing the rest of your clothes as he is ready to hold, kiss and make love to you.

From Flirting to Foreplay

Do not rush the foreplay, both men and women look forward to, and thoroughly enjoy, the excitement, sexiness, and feeling they get during foreplay. For women, this is usually the time your body needs to get ready for sex, so rushing it will not help. You may need to explain this to your husband. Be patient and direct so your husband will know what you need to feel connected and to fully enjoy sex.

Think about your favorite love-making experience, what did you like and how did you feel? Tell him all about it or show him. Let him know how much you desire to be with him. Let him know you think about sex and how it makes you feel. Make sure to let him know how much you want him to touch you, to kiss you, and make love to you.

There are actual chemical reactions that happen in the body when one is sexually aroused. Although I make no medical claims and this is not an anatomy lesson, but some research I have found useful suggests that having sex makes you happier and helps you fall deeper in love with your husband. Holding hands and other skin-to-skin contact decreases the stress hormone, cortisol, in the body. Having fun, dancing, kissing and spending time together increases the happiness hormone, oxytocin, in both men and women, and causes them to develop feelings of love and trust. As both partners become sexually aroused, more oxytocin is released which causes both men and women to want more touching. (Moberg, 2003)

Keep in mind that this is a very general outline of what happens to each of us and there is variation among individuals.

But in general, our bodies are literally programmed to respond to touching and caressing with love and trust. This is why flirting and foreplay are so vital to living the Girlfriend Effect.

Spending Time Together

*A*s you begin to live the Girlfriend Effect you need to make time to go out and do things together.

If you have not been spending time together you need to start with simply dating again, just like you did before you were married. Let me clarify dating by sharing an example of my client (name changed for privacy). Kim and her husband have been married for several years and do not have children yet. They are both building their careers and a business. A lot of the spare time at home is spent on business tasks, as they are both passionate about what they do. When I asked her how often they dated she replied about 3-4 times a month. I thought that was pretty good until I asked her what they did on those dates. Her reply was that most of the dating occurred within their circle of friends, so often the guys would be in one area while the girls talked in another area. Very rarely did they go on a date by themselves.

While going out with friends and attending social events is fun and exciting once in a while, so is dating each other in private. This gives you time to talk and share.

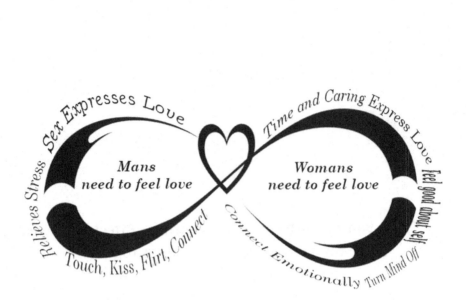

This private date time also allows you to become a better Girlfriend. One of your goals while dating is to keep your husband attracted to and paying attention to you with flirting and being there for him. I know this may sound like it's all about what your husband wants, but if you focus on being alone with him and spending time with him, you will become closer as you talk more, which leads to you feeling fulfilled, as well. Below are some simple steps to help your time together be more fun and exciting as you venture into the Girlfriend role.

Welcome home from work honey

Flirt with him all day by text or email, slip a note into his clothes before he leaves for work. Every couple of hours send him hints of what you have in mind for the evening just to get his attention. Just make sure you are ready for him when he gets home. (Might require some planning beforehand if you have kids.)

His choice tonight

He gets to choose what you will wear, but he has to go shopping with you to get it. Invite him on a lingerie shopping excursion to his favorite store. Let him buy anything he wants and you will wear it for him and reward his shopping efforts with a lap dance so you can model the new lingerie. Most men may not like clothes shopping, but if you offer him this opportunity he will be ready to shop without a second thought. (P.S. there are some stores that allow husbands into the dressing room area or have private areas. Take the opportunity for a fashion show, just don't get kicked out of the store.)

Another welcome home

Surprise your husband with an at-home sex date. Arrange for the kids to spend the night with friends or baby-sitter, then plan a romantic evening at home, no interruptions to worry about. Order in and have a romantic picnic in your room.

Plan to Play Naughty

It's cold outside but warm inside

Get outside your comfort zone, be a little daring. Make dinner arrangements. Wear your favorite outfit with lingerie underneath and give him hints of what you are wearing. If you feel like being really daring, wear a long coat with some sexy lingerie underneath or nothing at all. Throughout the night give him a hint or flash him some lace. He won't be able to concentrate the rest of the evening.

Relaxing on the weekend

Mention you are going to take a nap, but linger until you get his attention. Give him that look that says, 'I want you', but play a little hard to get. Text him that you need something in the other room, if this is out of the ordinary for you he may think something is wrong, but that's ok. (Make sure there is no one else in the house for this to work.) As you head to the bedroom start casually removing your clothes leaving a trail for him to find. By the time he enters the room be prepared to seduce him further with lingerie or no clothes. He just might decide he likes taking naps again.

Good morning

Secretly set the alarm clock to go off 30-40 minutes early to get all comfy and snuggle as you gently start to kiss his chest and neck. He may not be excited to wake up at first but whisper in his ear and let him know what you want. He will be happy to give you a great morning. There is no better way to start a day than having sex.

There's more ideas for having fun together later in the book. Whatever you choose to do, the important thing to remember that you need to make your relationship a priority. Find time to act like Girlfriend and Boyfriend and soon you will have those same feelings of excitement and love that existed before the wedding.

Cheering your Man on

*M*any women feel under-appreciated and uncared for because they think that they are not heard. The truth is that men feel the same way!

Too many times in a relationship, spouses are looking for what they personally need and want. They have not expressed this need to their partner but expect their partner to just know their desires. Part of this is miscommunication, or maybe there's no communication at all. When life is busy and couples are just rushing through life, they do not take the time to share how they honestly feel and what their expectations are. Additionally, some people do not know what they want, and thus cannot ask for it.

Take a few moments and decide what you really want from your man. Think about how you want him to touch, talk, kiss, and make love to you. Write it down so you can share this later. The main idea is that you want to do things for your husband, the very things YOU want in the relationship, WITHOUT any thought that you will get anything in return. This idea is perfectly simple. You give to your hubby what HE wants and eventually, HE will give back in return. Just try it!

If you are feeling underappreciated, give up on complaining and appreciate every little thing your husband does. IGNORE all the things that bug you. Pay close attention to everything he does from just the small simple things to big deal things: He helps around the house, He said I love you, He paid the bills. Even the little things you have divided up between yourselves. If it is considered HIS job, make sure to say thank you or good job. The idea is to give verbal acknowledgement of what HE did, without expecting anything in return.

I learned this a long time ago when trying to create a better atmosphere for my children and then I tried it on my husband, Mark, and it worked so well I have been using it ever since.

Once, on a very busy crazy day in our home full of teens and business I was feeling stressed and a little grumpy. I could tell that the rest of the family was feeling my attitude shift. I decided that instead of letting everything bug me I would only acknowledge the happy, creative, or nice things. Well, that was okay for a little while but soon I was complaining under my breath. One of my kids overheard and I realized that even though I was not outwardly voicing my displeasure, they could still sense my attitude.

I tried to gather my thoughts, so I could be happy; and though it was a forced happy, I was trying. My husband Mark came to see what was for dinner, and instead of barking an answer back at him I stated it would be a little while. I forced myself to hold in my emotions and did not point out that he wasn't helping and never did. Unfortunately yes, my attitude was still wavering. Instead, I decided to tell him that I loved him and said thank you for working so we could have food to eat. He was a little caught off guard by my response and then instead of going back to his home office as usual, he stayed out to play with our kids and talk.

This was a reaction I wanted to encourage.

That's when I knew I could change how people responded to me and how I could change the attitude of others around me. I still use this technique today in every relationship and it still works. Moral of my story, change your attitude to change the attitude of others!

Make this a habit with every relationship in your life and changes will happen within a few days. When you only notice the good things and verbalize it with praise and kindness, you will start to see the same in return. When you have an attitude of gratitude about what others do for you, it naturally encourages more of the same behavior. If you want your husband to truly listen to you, then you should be an active and attentive listener first. The behavior changes will result in a positive environment allowing more positive changes to occur.

JODI HARMAN

Making Him #1

ngoing communication throughout the day can help you both feel connected and strengthen feelings of love even when you are away from each other.

This does not mean that you should be the obnoxious girlfriend and call or text every 10 minutes or even that you should demand an answer right away. Remember, the idea of a text message or an email is that it will be answered when the receiver has time, not necessarily right away.

You are trying to create feelings of longing and thoughtfulness. Do not use this time for a complaining session or gripes about kids or coworkers. Keep it fun, light and sexy! Make the conversation about your spouse and let him know you care about how he is doing throughout the day.

As a Girlfriend, we work to hide the ugly parts of ourselves and our complaints of the day. Once we are married we stop hiding and share all aspects of our lives, or at least we should feel safe to do so. That is ok! But, there also needs to be time to go back to Girlfriend mode, time when we are only focused on the fun and happy parts of the relationship. Being in the role of Girlfriend should take you back to when there were fewer responsibilities, less stress and expectations. Let out your carefree spirit and have fun, relax and enjoy being together.

Another fun, and often forgotten, way to connect during the day is make a lunch date. This may not work for all couples but, if possible, you should try it once a week or month. Again, this is not a time to complain or have an emotional rollercoaster going on. This should be a time to break away from the busy day and just enjoy being with each other. If you need to communicate about family or work, try to keep it as a small portion of lunch and then focus on each other. As you depart from lunch with each other, take a few minutes to have an intense make out session. This can help set the mood for a rendezvous later in the evening. The anticipation can be intense and will help you both have a better day.

Below are some tips to help you start a conversation as you have your lunch date or other time together. This should not be a like a radio interview (unless you are role playing) but should allow you to discover new things about each other.

1. One of the funniest memories I have from when we first met is...
2. Do you remember when we first kissed, what was it like for you?
3. What was your first impression of me when we met?
4. The funniest memory I have from when we started dating is;
5. What is your most memorable date with me?
6. I have a memory of a certain outfit you were wearing;
7. What are some of your happiest memories with me?

8. What are some of your most sensual memories you have of us together?

9. Is there a time that you can think of that was embarrassing and we both just laughed at the end?

10. Do you remember the first words you said to me? Or the pick-up line you used?

11. Do you remember that dream of doing_____ we used to have? Should we still do it?

12. Do you have a favorite memory of _____ trip/ vacation we took?

13. If we could spend all day together, what would you like to do?

14. I have a vision of us in our older years, sitting on the porch in our rocking chairs. You look over at me and say, 'dang it, we never did _____'

15. If you could relive one of our best love making memories which one would you choose? Or, How many can you think of?

16. I remember a time I was scared to tell you something but when I did you were so kind; this is how I felt;

17. I love it when you say this to me;

18. I like it when you refer to me as;

19. My favorite wedding memory was...

20. My favorite memory of our honeymoon was...

For more conversation ideas, log onto
www.GirlfriendEffect.com.

You can use these topics as you start to wind down your day, too. Create a relaxation habit you can share with your husband that helps you both to disconnect from the day and reconnect with each other. The goal is to be together and sharing an experience. It could be watching TV, movies or playing video games, but the important part is to be present. Sitting in separate rooms does not count, this is not conducive to communication or making an emotional connection. Instead, take turns picking a show or movie and hang out together. Have a conversation during the commercials. Do not use the time to zone out or stare at your cell phone. Hold hands, cuddle, kiss, or have a full-blown make-out session during a movie, sit close and make 'roaming hands' fun again.

Watching television allows you to check out of the world and I AM CHALLENGING YOU TO CHECK BACK INTO YOUR MARRIAGE!

Communication That Fills
Emotional Needs

C ommon wife complaints: 'He never listens to me!' Or 'He doesn't care what I think!'

I used to be a wife who had these thoughts too. The truth is, men feel the same way! The actual problem is that neither of you are getting your emotional needs met and it makes you FEEL that you are not being heard, when in fact most men can repeat back to you the very thing you said a moment ago.

Feeling connected to your husband is the ultimate goal. I am sure you have heard the phrase, 'communication goes both ways.' To feel secure and loved both partners need to feel heard and understood. If you are feeling that your husband does not listen, this may lead you to giving up and not sharing at all. If this happens, you will lose the intimate connection that you both desire. Feelings of resentment, anger and frustration take the place of love and caring when partners are not communicating effectively. Additionally, constantly telling your man that he doesn't listen will just make the problem worse, because then he tunes you out and considers it nagging.

The relationship can go downhill very fast as the lack of communication causes you to not share your feelings, and in turn, your partner may develop feelings of mistrust. This sends the relationship off into a tail-spin as each partner gets defensive and starts to withdraw from all conversation, activities, and the relationship. It will not take long if communication does not improve, you will be more like roommates instead of partners and lovers.

When you do not feel heard and understood, you will feel that giving up may be easier or that you have no power to change things. The problem with these emotions and self-talk is that you DO have power over how you will behave and the things YOU will say. You only have control over yourself and that is where you need to start. Instead of blaming and punishing your husband, take an honest look at yourself and see what changes you can make that may help conversations turn out differently.

Communication is so much more than just talking. Talking is exchanging information and confirming facts, like "*What time will you be home?*" The kind of conversation every couple should have consists of sharing feelings, dreams, hopes, fears, and giving support. Honest, open communication fills an emotional need and innate desire to be heard, valued and loved.

Think of communication like a bank account. Would you rather have deposits or withdrawals? The same idea is true when you are having a meaningful, intimate conversation. When you were first married, you probably didn't think about this, but your actions showed it. Most newlyweds talk a lot and spend a lot of time together. You were making deposits into each other's account. You were putting your partner's needs above your own. This is emotional fulfillment.

Having your emotional needs met is vital to every human. Children will bug you until they get their emotional needs met. Think of a toddler that wiggles his way up your lap even though you are busy. He just wants to be held. Sometimes, as maturity sets in, adults have learned to stop asking and demanding that their emotional needs get met. That is why so many people are unhappy! When your emotional needs are met, that 'life-preserving' need is satisfied and you can then share it with others.

Emotional needs have different levels and can affect your mood accordingly. However, when a deep emotional need is met by your spouse, the one person that means everything to you, you feel euphoric, loved and cared for. This type of emotional caring and love is what a marriage is supposed to do for both partners in the relationship.

To make sure you are filling your husband's emotional needs, I suggest you ask some simple questions on a regular basis and then follow up with doing your best to fulfill the needs that are expressed.

'How can I be a better wife?'
'What can I do to help you?'
'What can I do to make you feel loved?'

This process alone can make a huge deposit into the emotional needs account. To improve the outcome of the conversation, consider telling your husband what it is going to be about in advance and the types of questions you are going to ask him. My husband is an analytical thinker, meaning he likes to think things through before he answers. Myself, I am a fast thinker and talker so I have a tendency to move too fast in conversations. Many marriages have different kinds of thinkers so you might find it helpful to let him know what you want to talk about either by verbally telling him or writing it down. This allows him time to think through the questions and come up with an answer. Especially the first couple of times you ask these questions, he may need time to ponder it a little.

Let's discuss what happens if you get an answer to the above questions that makes you feel upset or offended. In the next chapter I will cover some guidelines that we have found to be useful when these conversations need to take place. True, intimate conversation can happen when both parties view the process as a time to grow and learn to love each other more.

Intimate Conversation

*H*ave you ever felt that the person you were talking to was not actually listening to you or digesting what you were saying?

Many times, in conversations, people are not really listening to the person talking, but rather readying their response to what is being said. When it is a topic that all parties have a strong opinion on, neither can wait to share that opinion. Unfortunately, when this happens in a marriage relationship, one or both partners do not feel heard or understood and miscommunication is often the result.

Intimate Conversation allows both partners to verbally communicate feelings or opinions openly while the other person is intently listening, and then repeating it back for complete understanding and clarification.

During this conversation both need to be fully present, attentive and focused on what is being communicated, not preparing a response for when it is your turn to talk. Most people tend to get defensive when a serious conversation is about to happen, but this technique is not supposed to cause arguments. It is not a space to be mean or criticize each other, but to be open and clear with feelings and situations. Note: this technique should not be used solely for delicate or unpleasant conversations, it can be used anytime that you need your partner to understand you, from an argument to offering loving words of encouragement. For many, this may be the first time you have used this type of conversation technique and it is normal to feel vulnerable and uncomfortable. That said, the more you use it the more you will like it.

You must set aside a safe space within the relationship where there will be no judgment and no hurt feelings. There are two meanings when I mention the space:

> ***Physical Space*** *to have a conversation in private. (If you suspect the conversation may be unpleasant, try not to do it in your bedroom.)*
>
> ***Mental Space*** *that allows you to think with an open heart and mind, to have honest and pure conversations with each other free of judgment and anger.*

Communicating on an emotional level is one of the hardest parts of any relationship as each person was raised differently and usually has different communication styles. Most people tend to have communication styles patterned after one or both parents / caretakers from their youth. When couples get married, it is no wonder that communication is usually what causes the problem more than anything else in a marriage.

As you walk through the steps of having this conversation, stay open to your spouse's feelings as this will take you into deep conversations. Many times, spouses just need to accept and acknowledge what the other is saying. They need to make sure the other person is feeling heard. While the goal is to speak honestly and listen intently, it does not mean that you need to respond. This may be especially hard if you are a person who always has to get in the last word.

When conflicts occur with couples and neither is communicating, the partners tend to fall into one of two roles: running away and ignoring the problem, or getting comfortable with a long unloving relationship and seeing who can hold out the longest. The relationship begins to struggle, genuine caring is lessened, and sexual intimacy slows or halts as love begins to be lost. If left unchecked for too long, one or the other may look for love in another direction, choosing an affair or divorce, or they may choose to just live life as roommates. None of these options is pleasant.

In practice, this communication technique has been a great way for us to share both simple and complex conversations that would otherwise have ended with emotions out of control and hurt feelings.

Intimate Conversation

For Intimate Conversation there will be two people. You will decide which role each will have and then change roles as necessary.

The Communicator = Person Talking
The Receiver = Person Listening

The receiver only has two responses: Can you please repeat that? or Is there more to say?

Communicator: The conversation should start with the Communicator giving compliments and loving affirmations to the receiver. This helps to remove any uneasiness or defensiveness and allows free flowing love and appreciation for each other. This can be as simple as saying thank you for something the person has done, to a full-on dedication of love. When you say thank you and give compliments, most people are more inclined to do more of the same to get more appreciation. This is not a time for sarcasm or being mean, only love should flow.

Receiver: The receiver should repeat back what the communicator just said. For instance, if your spouse is the one speaking (communicator) and he just stated: *Thank you for making dinner for me, I really like it when I do not have to worry about that.*

You as the listener (receiver) you would internalize what was said and simple repeat it back to him like this: You said that you love that I made you dinner and you did not have to worry about it. Is there more? (asking this question allows the communicator to add more if he wants too) But you do not get to add anything further to the conversation. This is a one-way transfer of information only. It is about accepting what is being said, not a time to think of a retaliation or an argument back to what was just said.

The intimate conversation patterns are simple; it feels awkward at first because most people are not used to speaking this way. Intimate conversations allow for a transfer of information only. If the conversation is unpleasant or painful to either spouse, transfer the information and set a time for you to both ponder the information. Then, return to the dialog to clarify what has been shared, or simply take turns as communicator and receiver to work through for a resolution.

If you find that the transfer of information was not what you expected and one or the other has hurt feelings or is upset. Take a break as you ponder the information (moments, hours, days – hopefully not weeks – the sooner you revisit the conversation, the better). Then go back to the 'safe space' and take turns in each role of communicator and receiver as you share your feelings, remembering that the receiver can only respond in two ways. This keeps the information flowing and both partners have a chance to share and be heard.

You may use intimate conversation to talk about anything in your relationship. We have found it helpful to use it for subjects that need to be explained, may get confusing or emotionally negative, and even to discuss sexual preferences. As you practice this it will become easier and will not set off your defenses as much as when you first start.

Here's an example of how this can work. The following is an actual conversation we had several years ago:

We began by creating a safe space and decided who would be the communicator and who would be the receiver.

Jodi (communicator): I am so thankful that you work so hard to provide for our family. Thank you for loving me and supporting me

Mark (receiver): You are glad that I work hard and provide for the family. You also love that I love you and support you. Is there more?

Jodi (communicator): That is correct. I am struggling with time management and getting everything done. I need some help but do not feel like I can ask more of you.

Mark (receiver): You are having a hard time getting everything done and need me to help you more. Is there more?

Jodi (communicator): Yes, that is correct. Would you be willing to take over the responsibility of paying the bills and the budget? It is too hard for me right now and I think I paid a bill late.

Mark (receiver): You paid a bill late and need me to help by taking over paying bills and the budget. Is that all?

Jodi (communicator): I would like to get all the paperwork organized and let you take a look at it so you can see what I have been doing and where I need some help. I can have it ready tomorrow. Will that be ok? I don't think we should wait.

Mark (receiver): You want to get all the bills and paperwork organized and then show me what the problem is and would like to do that tomorrow. Yes, that will be ok. Is there more?

Jodi (communicator): Yes, that is all. Thank you for having this conversation. May we continue the conversation later?

Mark (receiver): You are happy we talked, and you do not have anything else to add. Yes, let me think about what you have said, and we will continue the conversation tomorrow evening.

END: We like to end our conversations with giving a long embracing hug and just saying *I love you* to each other.

The following day: I did a little preparation to be ready for the conversation and so did Mark, as you will see. This time Mark will be the communicator and I will be the receiver. Honestly, I was a little apprehensive to continue the conversation because I knew he must be disappointed or upset about paying a late fee. I also knew that his work was really busy at the time and he probably did not need the added pressure or responsibility. This is what happened:

Mark (communicator): Thank you for being a good mom and taking care of the family. Thank you for taking care of the bills for this whole time and now reaching out for help. I love you.

Jodi (receiver): I am a good mom and do a good job of taking care of the family. You are glad that I have had the responsibility of taking care of the bills, and you love me. Is that all?

Mark (communicator): There is more. After analyzing what we discussed yesterday I think we should set some time aside every week for about an hour and go over the budget and bills together. Will that solve the problem? I do not think I have time to do it myself, but we should do it together.

Jodi (receiver): You have looked at your personal time and think it would be a good idea if we work on the budget together. You want me to help you and think that will be best. Is there more?

Mark (communicator): Yes, Can you show me the bill that was paid late and what the problem is? Did we get penalized for the late payment?

Jodi (receiver): You want to the see the bill that was late. The problem was that I forgot to pay it. Yes, there was a late payment fee. (I then showed him the bills and the penalty)

Mark (communicator): I think if we do this together on the weekend it won't be overwhelming for either of us. If I am out of town you will need to take care it on your own, but we can talk on the phone. Will this work?

Jodi (receiver): You want to spend time on the weekend to go over the bills and budget. If you are not home on the weekend you would like me to take care of it and can talk to you on the phone. Is there more?

Mark (communicator): No, I think this will work. I love you. Thank you for talking with me and being willing to share the responsibility.

END: we both hug and say I love you. We then took the time to pay bills together. As we reflected on this conversation, we both felt that we could say what the problem was and had a chance to share our concerns with time management.

Personally, I am so glad that Mark did not get upset about me paying a bill late. In the past, this probably would have ended in an argument, I am grateful that he loves me enough to have this type of conversation. It allows you a break from what you are feeling (anger, hurt) because you do not get to say any of that. Then after you have pondered and come to terms with a logical conclusion you get to talk again. It is the ideal way to get to the bottom of anything that you need to discuss.

The most important part of this process is that the receiver cannot retaliate or respond in a negative way. The receiver will only repeat back and process the information. This will cause some self-reflection for both parties and may even make them uncomfortable. The receiver may need to apologize and that does not have to take place at the very moment, but a new intimate conversation may need to take place at another time when both are ready for it. Working through this process may take time but can create great bonds of closeness and allow for partners to connect more deeply.

Truly accepting your partner is the deepest form of love and happiness you can wish for. You must be willing to accept what your partner says. It does not mean that you agree with what they said or that you even understand it all right now. Just ACCEPT the information, process it and decide what needs to be done in the future. This may mean behaviors need to change or thought processes need to change, but that comes later. Acceptance is just simply receiving and hearing what was said.

This is not a chance to change your partner, but rather giving yourselves the opportunity to examine your inner feelings. Many times, when people are unhappy they look outwardly to find the cause of the unhappiness. Before you try to blame or change anyone else, take a look inside yourself. If you are not willing to change yourself, do not expect change in your partner. Being willing to accept them for who they are is better than trying to change them. For some people pride and ego may get in the way. You need to be accepting of yourself and others in all relationships including: friends, children, parents, and others. Too often, judgment of others happens before self-evaluation, thus leading to an unhappy ending.

People interpret things differently. For instance, within a family situation you will have different personalities and communication (both talking and listening) is different for each person. Becoming aware of what you want to say before it is released from your mouth is ideal for every conversation. An additional lesson I learned was, not everything you think needs to come out of your mouth. Remember Thumper's mother from the movie Bambi, 'If you do not have anything nice to say, don't say anything at all.' I learned this at a very early age, as the home I grew up in was very negative and not very many nice things were said. I vowed then that I would be cautious about what I said. Too many times people just say what they are thinking.

Remember, the words you say cannot be taken back. You may apologize, but the words were still spoken.

Sarcasm is a way to say something that should not have been said. There is NO PLACE for this in marriage. Soon, one or both of the spouses halts all communication as the sarcasm has created a habit of shutting down the emotional needs of the other person. The intimate conversation helps to retrain each person to have open, deep conversations. The acknowledgement of ACCEPTANCE brings love and value to the communicator.

Do not blow off your partner's comments or imply comments that are unnecessary or not true feelings, as this can take away from self-worth and lowers the value of the relationship bank account. When this happens, it leaves the offended spouse feeling as if there is no value to their thoughts, feelings and emotions. When using the intimate communication, it allows both partners to process the information that was delivered and validate how they think, feel and believe; this adds value to the relationship creating a strong emotional bond.

If communication is a problem within the marriage, it will begin to create walls and cause people to shut down and not communicate any longer. You need to be open to talk with each other. It needs to be okay for each person to share their feelings, without the other person taking offense or judging them. However, the person talking may need to adjust how the message is delivered. Taking the necessary time to think about what you want to say and how it might be perceived will be vital to the person receiving the message. Remember, the communicator in the conversation may have pent up resentment or hurt feelings about what they are about to say. However, the message should be delivered without feelings being attached. This is hard to do if it is a heated subject, but it will be necessary to carry out the conversation in a way that does not place blame or hurt onto the receiver. It may be best to relay information after anger has calmed.

Silence does not help a relationship; it causes a bigger divide between you. Besides if you will just start, it makes it easier. Trust me! There have been times when we weren't talking and we have been able to break past those barriers.

Having conversations like this is not always pleasant and for many couples this would have caused an argument instead of creating a safe, growing place to learn how to communicate with each other. You should not take an offence at what is being said. If the receiver is feeling upset with information received, that just means that perhaps some soul-searching may need to take place to analyze the situation. The person receiving should be open to truly listen to what the other person is saying. Acceptance may not always happen right at once; sometimes it may take several days for them to come around, and to fully understand what the person was saying and was not meant to cause harm to the relationship.

Allowing intimate conversations to be common place in your relationship means that there will be fewer disagreements, more sharing, and more love felt by both partners. This does not mean that you will not talk about events and situations that need to be discussed to run a household.

Now you have a way to have a conversation that is nonjudgmental and loving and be able to heal your relationship.

Break Bad Habits

Why Women Love So Well, But Don't Ask for Love in Return

omen are experts at giving love and have the inborn desire and ability to care for people.

Far too many times, I hear women complain about their husband for the exact things that we are experts at. Ladies, we are amazing at giving love and affection, and that is what men need and want. However, we forget to tell them what we want in a way that they can understand. Many times women go through life expecting their husband to just know what they want and need.

Knowing how to ask for what you want and need in the relationship will be a huge step forward. If you can get better at asking, it may have the power to change the dynamics of your marriage. I am sure you have heard of the book, *Men are From Mars, Women are from Venus* by John Gray. He perfectly describes the major communication problem facing every relationship: men and women speak differently and understand differently.

Here's an example, one that I bet will be familiar to most readers. I remember one crazy day when we had a busy family and I asked my husband to stop at the store to get some milk and anything else he wanted to have in his lunches for the week. He came home with only the milk. I was perplexed as to where the snacks, bread and chips were that I was sure he would want in a few days. He replied that he did what I asked and got milk. I accepted that but then went on to be upset the rest of the evening because now I was going to have to fit in a trip to the store within a few days.

Come to find out later, my hubby did not even know I was mad, he thought the conversation was over because I had not said anything else. As I thought about the situation, I realized I did not share my expectations very well, then got mad that he didn't read my mind. Even typing this now, years later, I wonder how he was supposed to read my mind. I wish I had this book back then, life would have been so much better.

I want you to make a list of all the things that your husband does that lets you know you are loved and appreciated. Keep this list handy and over the next couple of days – I want you to really think about it and make a long list, even if it is something he used to do but not so much anymore, write it down.

I know some of you can only fill up the opposite list of what he does that does NOT make you feel loved. If you feel you need to make this list as well, that is fine, but we are not going to be sharing that with anyone, instead it will be used as a reference as you work through the next steps in the process.

Take a look at the list with all the things he does that does NOT convey love. See what you can do to make the items into a statement to tell your husband what you need. Here are a few examples of how you can change common complaints into asking for love.

If he leaves his clothes out all over the floor and that bothers you, I want you to write: I feel loved when you (husband) clean up after yourself.

If he does not help around the house, I want you to write: I feel loved when you help me around the house.

If he forgets to say I love you often, I want you to write: I feel loved when you tell me you love me.

Continue to work on this list and describe how you feel loved when he does specific things.

On your next date night, I want you to share some of the things he does that make you feel loved. He will not know unless you tell him. Remember you only get to tell him;

I feel loved when you _____.

To make sure you are both asking for the love you want, ask your husband if he would like to make this list with you and then take turns sharing your I feel loved when you... statements.

Making the Relationship a Priority

*H*ow much time are you spending with each other? What are you doing during this time?

When I talk with clients or friends about how much time they spend with family and then alone with their husbands. I am always a little shocked by their answers, though it seems to go right along with the average America family.

According to the U.S. Department of Labor and Statistics (2014), the average American spends about one to two hours a day caring and spending time with others. If your household has children, there is good and bad news for the marriage relationship. Unfortunately, the children will take up most of this time and attention, possibly leaving little-to-no time for your marriage. The report also stated time spent on recreation and sports to be approximately two hours per day. This could be for yourself, spouse or kids. Personally, when I exercise or go to the gym it is usually about one to one and one half hours. If you add eight to nine hours for work and a few hours for sleep, that makes for a full day. If your life is this busy and full, how do you find time for each other?

I have a friend that confided in me she was having marital problems and both she and her husband were not happy. I asked her how much time they spent together, and she professed about one to two hours a day. With that answer I had to know more. Come to find out, the majority of the time they were spending together was at their children's sporting events. Sitting in the stands watching and talking with friends, or at times helping in the snack booth.

It was not hard to see why they were not feeling connected. The time they did spend together was for their kids, about their kids, or volunteering, but not focused on each other. By the time they got home, got the kids fed, homework done, and everyone settled, they were both so exhausted they hardly spent any intimate time together, though they did manage to fit in a quickie once in a while.

If you go to a child's sporting event to support your child, that is not considered a date - that is family time. Spending time on your relationship does not involve anyone but the two of you. Plan time to go on a date where there are no children and you can both focus on each other. Knowing that you will have time together soon helps you get through the week. Again, put your marriage first and life will still happen, but you will both be happier about it all. My friend implemented the tips and ideas in this book and I can happily say that they are still busy as ever, AND their marriage is better.

My husband and I have several businesses and have always been self-employed. We have an office at the house, something that is very common nowadays. Unfortunately in the past, we often worked a lot, especially late in the evening. This left us physically and emotionally drained from too much work. We have found that blocking time and setting boundaries for work and play help make our relationship the most important part of us. If we go to bed at the same time, it helps us to connect with each other. We have also had to leave work outside our bedroom door. Even now, we go on dates and start to talk about business, but can quickly recognize this and stop.

Becoming stuck in the mom role happens to most women when they start a family. A lot of women stop thinking of themselves as a 'sexy woman' once they start having children, whether because of body changes or family demands or both. The feeling of being a Girlfriend can dissipate over time. The sexual relationship gets put to the side because women (and men) forget to put their relationship first, which sabotages the relationship. Having a balanced role of mother and sexy wife is required.

When you are on a date you should be talking about the relationship, not the kids, house, money, or other responsibilities. This may be an eye-opening experience for some people as they realize that the amount of time they spend on their relationship is very small when these things are taken out. Just talk to each other about goals, dreams, and aspirations. Ask your husband, how are you? Then just talk.

Break it down into hours, how many hours do you spend on your relationship. How much time are you spending focused on your husband? Whether or not you have a family, most couples spend very little time on the marriage relationship, often just enough for survival. If you want your marriage to thrive, your quality time - YOU NEED MORE! Check out where you are spending your time. How does this impact your relationship? Are there some places in your life that you feel you can cut out or simplify to make room for your marriage?

"The American Time Use Survey collects information about the activities people do during the day and how much time they spend doing them... Employed persons ages 25 to 54, who live in households with children under 18, spent an average of 8.9 hours working or in work-related activities, 7.7 hours sleeping, 2.5 hours doing leisure and sports activities, and 1.2 hours caring for others, including children."

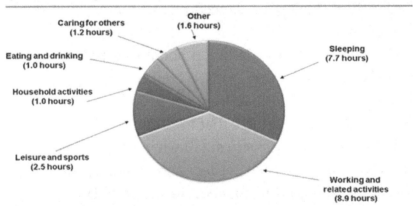

Time use on an average work day for employed persons ages 25 to 54 with children

Caring for others (1.2 hours)

Other (1.6 hours)

Eating and drinking (1.0 hours)

Sleeping (7.7 hours)

Household activities (1.0 hours)

Leisure and sports (2.5 hours)

Working and related activities (8.9 hours)

NOTE: Data include employed persons on days they worked, ages 25 to 54, who lived in households with children under 18. Data include non-holiday weekdays and are annual averages for 2014. Data include related travel for each activity.
SOURCE: Bureau of Labor Statistics, American Time Use Survey

- US Department of Labor American Time Use Survey (US Bureau of Labor Statistics, 2014)

According to the chart above, we each have about seven hours each day when we are not sleeping or working. Of course, there are a lot of things that have to get done during that time - meals must be prepared, laundry must be done, toilets must be scrubbed - but there's also a lot of time available to care for yourself, your children, AND your husband.

The idea is to examine your life and determine where you are spending your time. Are there some activities you can adjust to make more room for your marriage?

It is too easy to let the day-to-day running around with family and career take over your time. Many people run from one thing to the next, even multi-tasking to get more done in a day. The problem with all the hustle and bustle is that too many couples put their relationship last. In other words, they do not think about spending time with each other until the late evening hours, after all your energy has been zapped away. This leaves little energy and focus for one of the most important persons in your life, your husband.

As you live the Girlfriend Effect one of the things your husband should notice right away is that you are paying attention to him as he becomes a priority to you.

Defining Your Roles in Life

*I*t might be overwhelming to think about how in the world you are going to be able to be in The Girlfriend role and succeed at everything else that you are doing. It may take work at first, but once you begin to create new habits, it will just be what you do every day.

Life almost requires you to change roles on a minute-to-minute basis. Occasionally, when you are in the mom or businesswoman role, it can be hard to also be a sexy girlfriend. I think our men understand about being in these roles, especially the mom role. There will be times that you cannot be sexy in the clothes you wear, but you can always have confidence and attitude.

From time to time, the role of parent can get in the way of being a friend and lover with your man. Don't let yourself get caught in that trap!

Four Rules If You Have Kids

1. Do not let children sleep in your bed! I've been there, I know it is hard to be a mom one minute and then a hot, sexy wife the next. You are always thinking of what needs to be done around the house or you are tired from being up at night with babies.

When I was a new mom, I was so tired all the time and thought it would be a good idea to just let the baby sleep with us so I did not have to get up so much, plus the baby slept better. Little did I know this was causing some jealousy with my husband! He missed being able to touch me and sleep next to me. He was so patient and did not say anything for a time. Eventually, I came around and realized I missed him too. The baby was then taken to his/her own bed and we got to spend that little bit of time together again. As the kids got older, I remember making a small little area with big stuffed animals next to the child's bed. If they awoke in the night, I went to their room and lay down next to their bed until they fell asleep. Awaking sometimes with a stiff neck was better than dividing my marriage with a child in the middle of my bed. I made it a point to always sleep next to my husband. One of the best feelings after being up with a child at night, is climbing into bed to snuggle up with my hubby.

2. You must remember to touch each other. All too often, moms are the primary caregiver and get most of their touch, love and attention needs met by the children. Women can even begin to feel as if they have been touched too much. They feel overwhelmed with all the needs of everyone in the family. They feel tired and drained and just want some quiet time alone. Dads get left out in the cold (literally) with little to no touching or cuddling and they begin to resent the time and attention the kids get. We need to remember that men need to be touched, caressed and loved too.

3. We always tried to go to bed at the same time too. At times, one of us would be waiting for the other but we decided to

make this a priority. We both look forward to this time to connect and just be together. It is also more likely to lead to making love since you are conversing, cuddling and enjoying each other's company.

4. Never go to bed angry. I remember when I first got married, my new mother-in-law told us to never go to bed angry. Anger allows the resentment and frustration to fester and as usual there is little communication and a lot of hurt feelings and very little sleep on these nights. When feelings like this are allowed to continue the mind can play tricks on you and you start to think more negatively about your spouse. As you toss and turn you will be thinking about all the things the other has done that bugs you, or previous disagreements will invade your thoughts, preventing sleep further. If there is no way for a simple or fast resolution to the problem but you must sleep, at least say I love you and hold each other. You might be surprised how this alone can change feelings.

Stuck in the Mom Role

Being stuck in the mom role can take its toll on all relationships, not just marriage. As women, we are natural caretakers and are usually pretty good at juggling all the responsibilities this entails. Although this is not a parenting book, I give you permission to get a babysitter and do something for yourself. Not only will this make you a better wife and lover, you will also be a better mom.

Clothes

Having babies changes the shape of your body, usually accentuating your curves a little more. When women are in the mom role we tend to wear clothes that are serviceable and it doesn't matter how they fit because the clothes will get dirty with food stains or handprints. I made sure that by the time my husband got home I was changed into something more appealing and attractive.

Make sure you have a few changes of clothes you can easily slip into that makes you feel better about how you look. For instance, I remember getting a new pair of white Gap jeans, my favorite. It wasn't long before I had dirty handprints right on my butt. But I had bleach and knew it was ok.

Exercise

Being a mom takes a lot of energy and patience, all on very little sleep. If you want to improve your mood, your body, your mind, and your sleep; get some regular exercise. I know this sounds like one more thing to do, but your body releases endorphins when you exercise, these are the very hormones you need to help you feel sexy, plus, you will have more energy.

Do some homework to see which gyms in your area offer childcare. When I had young ones at home I got together with some friends and let the kids play while we exercised. Even taking the kids to the park can turn into exercise. Put the kids in a stroller or wagon or bike seat, let them know this time is yours and when you get to the park they are free to get out and have fun.

Thoughts

Get your mind and language out of mommy talk by reading a book, watching a movie, or finding a new hobby. This is not meant to add more stress, but your mind needs to be challenged just as much as your body needs to be moved. Taking some time to do something just for you will give you the break you need.

Adult time

Mommies have play dates because the kids need to socialize. However, mommies need time with friends too. You should get a sitter or trade with a friend so you can go out without your kids. Get dressed up and meet a friend or your hubby for lunch. This gives you something to look forward too and gives you a break. Have friends over for a game or just to talk. Warning: if they bring their kids your house will be a mess by the time they all leave and you will spend the rest of the day cleaning. I recommend going to the park or somewhere besides your home, if possible, since the added stress may counteract the enjoyment.

Flirt

You might need to remember how to do this again if you have been in the mom role for too long. I have added a whole chapter for you to have fun with! Flirting with your husband will definitely give you the boost of confidence you may lack when bogged down with daily household activities.

For the career-driven woman

Stop thinking about the boardroom and move into the bedroom. Pick a time that makes sense for you to disconnect from work. Depending on your job, you may need to check emails or return calls after normal work hours, but recognize that setting boundaries is healthy, too.

I often have to remind myself that just because I can do something, it doesn't mean that I always should. Yes, I am talking about being so driven in your business that you forget about your marriage. Earlier I talked about scheduling time for dates, communication, and even sex. For so long, women have worked to prove themselves in the business world that we have become constantly wired up for work and thrive on the adrenaline rush of being needed.

This ambition may help you climb the corporate ladder or help you succeed in your career but don't forget that you also have a husband to please! I have been guilty of this on occasion, especially if I'm up against a deadline. Don't be afraid to say NO; there is power in No!

Shutting down the businesswoman in you, and all the electronics, to leave work at work is a challenge. Many of us now find ourselves stuck bringing work home with us. So how do you 'flip the switch' from work to sexy wife to give your husband the Girlfriend experience he desires? Take a moment to think about what matters most.

If you are trying to remember everything you need to do, your brain acts like a computer that is running too many programs at the same time, eventually it shuts down because it's too busy or it runs super slow. Try making a list of all the things you didn't get finished. Put the list where you will see it first thing the next day, then forget about it. The unfinished projects you have are the open programs, once closed you can concentrate on things that matter, like your husband. Freeing your mind of the things on your list will make time and energy available to be creative and bring the Girlfriend experience into reality.

When you are done working try turning off all electronics, including your cell phone. Make it a point to have real conversations with other people about things other than work. Many people, myself included have their phone next to their bed. In our home, it is the main phone source for the household, the mother in me wants to know that if I am needed they will be able to reach me. I recommend that you at least turn the phone to silent so you are not bothered by work. Cell phones and computers buzzing during sex is a distraction and a romance buzz kill. Make sure to put it away. If you need to be available for family members, remember it is for emergency only late at night or while talking with your hubby.

I have even found it helpful to actually change out of work clothes when arriving home, however do not put on your old sweat pants and t-shirt. Put on a little sexy dress or jeans and nice blouse to help you feel beautiful. Looking and feeling sexy will attract your man while creating a more sexual response in yourself. I also know that men love it when you cook dinner all dressed up and in high heels - warning, be prepared for flirting and fun.

A few other things that may help you switch roles from career woman to sexy wife. Exercise and meditation may help some, while others will need more help than that. Light some candles and take a bath, spend a romantic moment by yourself.

Do you remember what life was like before you had the responsibilities of family, kids, career, and life? When you were the Girlfriend you would get ready to spend time with your boyfriend. The anticipation and flutters of the unknown encounter that may occur when you see each other were so exciting.

I remember as a teenager spending an hour in the bathroom reapplying my makeup and fixing my hair just to meet my boyfriend down at the park so we could hang out and talk. Think back to the time when you were the Girlfriend before you were married; Even if it was just dinner at his place or watching television together, you would have changed clothes, checked your hair and makeup, and generally looked forward to the evening. Even a mundane night in was fun and exciting.

Now, as you are in the role of the Girlfriend again, make sure you still give as much time and attention to seeing him.

How a Girlfriend Shows Up
Everyday

Girlfriend is a woman that is sexy, loves herself, is sexually confident and wants to radiate that view of herself to everything in life.

Be the woman that shows up prepared to be who she really is. Take the necessary time to get ready for the day, and ready to take on anything that comes your way.

A Girlfriend enjoys exercise and taking care of herself, I am not a fitness trainer but I can tell you from personal experience that when I exercise, my body releases chemicals called endorphins and adrenaline. Theses hormones change your mood and help you to be happy. Not just that, but when you exercise and build muscle, when you are moving your body, you will feel better about yourself. Some people call exercise a necessary evil, but if you find something you like to do it won't be that bad.

What you wear and how you show up

Feeling good in the clothes you wear is imperative to how you show up. Honestly answer these questions: What's in your closet? When was the last time you went shopping? When you go shopping for clothes are you just getting whatever you find for a cheap price or are you shopping for clothes that make you feel amazing and powerful? (I understand that sometimes cost may be an issue, but try to look your best.)

Get dressed and primped to present yourself. Be conscious of what you wear. Clothes make a statement. Do you dress like a mom, business woman, just back from gym (all day), old t-shirt and baggy jeans? What are you wearing right now?

Self-Care is a **Necessity & Priority** **Not Just a Luxury**

I want you to take inventory of what is in your closet. Try everything on and look in a full-length mirror. If you do not feel like a '10' in it, donate it or get rid of it. Then start making a list of things you need so you are ready for the next time you go shopping.

Your clothes should say, "I feel good about myself. I am excited about who I am. I am confident in who I am. I want to look good. I feel great and am present." In life you need to show up confident and sexy! This is not just about looks; your clothes can determine how you feel about yourself and how others treat you. Think about the shopping scenes from the movie, *Pretty Woman*, a change of outfit made for a change in attitude. Let your husband know that you care about yourself enough to take the time to look good. Your man will love this and be more attracted to you!

Do's and don'ts of dressing like a Girlfriend

I know there are different things that you need to dress for; such as being a mom, work, being social, church, etc. A Girlfriend dresses appropriately for each event but still possesses a sex appeal that cannot be ignored.

Let's do an experiment; go put on your favorite outfit, one that makes you feel like you are on top of the world. Look at yourself in the mirror. Look at the way it shows off your curves, and just enjoy the feelings you have when you wear it. You can feel this way every day with some attention to what you put in your closet.

Jeans and T-shirt kind of day: Jeans can make your butt look great if you get the right fit for your body type. Take some time to go to the mall and try on several brands. Actually, look in the mirror at your butt. Determine what looks good on you and buy plenty. Look for t-shirts that complement your figure. Try different necklines and pay attention to how the fabric feels against your skin. When you know what looks good on you, what makes you feel good about yourself, you can stock up and always feel gorgeous.

The right outfit can change how a woman feels about herself

Now let's talk about dresses and skirts: The same applies to dresses and skirts. Pay attention to what you are purchasing. Wearing a dress for comfort is ok as long as it looks good too. There are so many body types, it is important that you try on several styles and brands until you find the ones that make you feel amazing. I personally love to wear dresses and heels. I feel sexy and confident when I wear a dress so I make sure I have a ton of dresses and plenty of cute shoes to go with each. If you do not have a budget for this, simply find a few items (dresses, skirts, blouses) that can be matched up well and wear them often. I promise it will change how you feel about yourself. If you show up in life well-dressed and confident, others notice. You will get compliments and your self-esteem will sky rocket. You will be on your way to being the Girlfriend your husband is looking for and always wanted.

PS: Did you know that what you wear impacts how you feel about yourself and can either elevate your mood or depress you. The following quote is from a study of men's attire, but it illustrates the point.

'Clothing communicates information about the wearer and first impressions can be heavily influenced by the messages conveyed by attire. The man was rated more positively on all attributes. It went on to add, men may be advised to purchase clothing that is well-tailored, as it can positively enhance the image they communicate to others.' (Howlett, Pine. et al., 2013)

Although this quote talks about men, the same can be said for women. Well-tailored clothes can positively enhance the image you present to others, especially your husband.

Let's Have Some Fun

Secrets To Making Love More

 quandary of how much sex is too much for women and how much is too little for men is a question society has been trying to answer for decades.

A better question would be, "How much love, attention and sex does each partner in the marriage need to feel fulfilled?" With differing impulses and desires for each person, how does a couple decide what is right for them and keep both partners happy? I know when both partners are putting the relationship first, this problem is often solved as increased intimacy occurs naturally.

For those couples struggling with different levels of desire and need for sex, maybe this will help take your sex life from ordinary to fulfillment. Try the following ideas and see what works for your

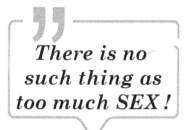

There is no such thing as too much SEX !

relationship and perhaps implement them one at a time. When you are ready to make more improvements and increase sexual intimacy, add in another idea from this book.

The biggest deterrent to having more sex is time. With the demands of life, work, and family, sex is often the last thing on your mind, especially for women. Without sex as a priority, couples can often go days, weeks, even months with little to no intimate contact, let alone sex. So whether you are having once a week or everyday there is always the possibility of more, or at least a better quality level of intimacy.

Choose how much

Move your relationship to number one on your list, with intimacy and sex right along with it. Most people have goals for other areas of their life, especially in business. I would like you to set a goal for your sex life. Simply decide, at first, to increase your intimate time one more time than what you are currently at. As you ease into this new goal, decide when to increase it again. Ultimately couples should be spending intimate time together 4-5 days a week, if you are living the Girlfriend Effect. This will vary for each couple so be flexible and you will find what works best for your particular life. Find out what each of you prefer and then mutually decide how many times you will have sex each week.

You may also choose to change it up from week to week as you figure out what works for each of you. If you decide together it can be a different number each week. Use your creativity when deciding how much and when you will fulfill this commitment. Be open to different times of the day and be willing to be adventurous. If your goal is four times a week and it's Thursday, get creative on how to get in an extra rendezvous. It becomes a lot of fun, and possibly a competition, as you are both thinking about sex all week. To some, this will feel like the spontaneity of your sexual encounters will be ruined, but the goal is to increase how much intimate time and sex you are having. Ultimately, the amount of sex and how much you enjoy sex is individual for each couple, so take the time to figure out what works for you. Have fun and be spontaneous, but more than anything, just do it.

You've made the commitment; Now what?

Now that you have made the commitment to each other to have sex more and touch each other more, you have to take action to strike up the mood, or it's not just going to happen. Too often couples wait until they are in the mood to even think about having sex, thus the waiting period from the past. If you struggle to get in the mood, try to think about the times that you have had hot spicy sex with your man. Think about it until you can feel the same feeling arise in you again. Picture your man without any clothes on. Now, play out the last time you had a really great make out session. Think about some fantasy that you want to introduce. Take full advantage of your imagination. Remembering the good times will help you get in the mood, but it will also draw you closer to each other.

Who's in charge

Although *The Girlfriend Effect* is written for women, that does not mean you must do all the planning for date nights, intimacy and fun. Once you have decided on how and when to increase your dates and sexual encounters, decide who will be in charge of which nights. The goal is to share the responsibility of preparing and making arrangements, if needed. Usually, I find that men are the ones that do most of the planning in this department so I am asking women to come forward and help. It does not always have to be one partner initiating and taking charge of the sexual relationship.

Once you set your intimacy goals I want you to each take turns in planning out the encounters. For instance, if you know that Fridays are a really busy day at work for your hubby then you should plan the intimacy time that day. If Mondays are rough, you may choose to make that a day off (if you are taking a day off). The idea of taking turns will make your hubby happier, as there will be less pressure on him. The thrill of not knowing what is going to happen is exciting and can enhance the intimacy.

Keep him guessing

Intimacy is not just a bedtime routine

Intimacy and sex do not have to be a bedtime event! Couples stuck in the bedtime routines of sex-then-sleep have created this habit. Habits can be changed. Sex and intimacy can happen at any time of day and just about anywhere (try not to get arrested).

You might just decide that another time of day is more erotic and exciting, once you open yourselves to the possibilities. Maybe as soon as you get home from work or when you wake up in the morning, switching it up adds to the spontaneity of the encounters. Weekends open up all sorts of opportunities for different places and times to throw caution to the wind.

Be adventurous! I think one of my favorite memories was a hike in the mountains when we stepped off the path for a picnic lunch and found solitude in a grove of trees for some adventurous sexual folly. Just the fact that you are willing to be adventurous at different times of the day will ignite new ideas and your husband will be ecstatic. Be imaginative with your time.

Sex is always a good idea

Set the mood with the right music

Music can change any mood within moments and you should use this to your advantage. If you both like a different genre, then either take turns or compromise on something that you both like. Pay attention to the music that you do not like or that is distracting to either one or the other of you, as this will not set the mood you are hoping for. Additionally, I prefer my music not to be too loud as that can be a mood killer. The music should help bring you closer and give you the ability to have conversations and be close with each other as it sets the mood.

Hint: My husband is such a romantic that he actually took the time to make a playlist mixing up his and my favorite music to help set the mood. (Doesn't that sound exactly like something you did when you were a teenage boyfriend/ girlfriend.) I was so excited to find that my husband surprised me with a soundtrack he made with some of our favorite music. He even put them in a specific order as to how the intimacy can grow as we spent the evening together.

Sex can fix anything

Enough with the excuses, there is always time for sex. There is no better way to stop just about any argument or disagreement than to have sex. Just try flirting, it can negate wı. ever is going on. The excuse of being too tired or too stressed to have sex is also incorrect.

Sex is a form of exercise and can actually give you more energy and improve your mood. There are way too many excuses and reasons to put off slipping into the sack. To give yourself a boost of energy and happiness you need to be having sex as much as possible. Living the Girlfriend Effect will help with those times when emotions and arguments bubble up, a sexual encounter may help diffuse a situation and make you both more agreeable to another point of view.

Keep your sex life smoldering all day

Couples who are in the Girlfriend and Boyfriend roles are constantly thinking of each other and do not keep the fire just in the bedroom. Keeping your husband at the forefront of your mind will heighten your sense of desire, which makes you want to be with him 24/7. This increases the intimacy and amount of sex you are having. Follow the examples in the flirting and getting in the mood chapters. The whole idea is that you think about you and your man having sex more often.

Pamper yourself to feel sexy

As the busyness of the day and family life can leave you feeling exhausted and we often put our own needs last. Take some time to pamper yourself and it will help you feel attractive, beautiful and sexy. Try getting a manicure and pedicure (or do it yourself), Take a long bath to relax and refresh. Get a massage or ask your hubby for one (usually this helps you both relax and get in the mood). Do some yoga or stretches to help relax after a long day. Mediation is usually my favorite to relax and unwind. This could even be as simple as taking a quick shower. Also give yourself a facial right before bed, brush your teeth and put on your favorite lotion or essential oil. There are several essential oils that can also help with relaxation, stress, and to help you get in the mood.

Don't think of Sex as a chore

Couples who have sex often know that no matter what kind of sex you have it is amazing: from a quickie to satisfy without a lot of preparation to an intimate night of romance with all the fireworks. Having a quickie or one person giving oral sex without the expectation of more can be enough sometimes. No need for wild gymnastics and hours of groping every single day. A quickie is fun because you know there will be more tomorrow or the next day. The goal is to be intimate and have sex more often. Sex is amazing no matter what!

Delirious Without Desire

How to Get in the Mood When Nothing Works

$\mathcal{I}$ am sure you can think of many reasons to reach for the remote control or a pillow instead of having sex. Or perhaps both you and your hubby have fallen into routines that consist of not considering sex as a priority.

Life is stressful, but you need to find some ways that can help you get in the mood. Remember, if it is important to you then you will find time! Turning it on and turning it off will be easier if you develop habits that will get you in the right frame of mind. If you are used to getting ready for bed in a specific way and grabbing the same old pajamas, it is time to change it up. Here's a few hints to help you get in the mood when you just don't feel like it.

1. The same old routine

Most people get though life by having routines and that is usually ok, except for when you become bored or complacent. It is often easier to stay in the routine than to make changes. If your bedtime routine is simply to wash your face, brush teeth, change into the old comfortable pajamas, slide into bed and relax by using electronics (TV/social media/games), it's time to take a look at *why* this is your routine.

Did you know that there is an actual chemical change that occurs in your brain when you do something new? Think about when you go on vacation and stay in a hotel. Many people become more relaxed and sleep better. Another reason to go on vacation is because sex is always more fun and exciting. These changes in routine create different feelings.

It is time to break the routine. Instead may I suggest: brush your teeth, fix your hair and slip on something sexy; then slide into bed and surprise your hubby. The change in behavior and routine will ignite passion and help you get in the mood.

2. You are too tired or have too much to do

The problem is that you are putting your relationship last, you wait until the end of the day when you have no energy and the demands of the day have used all your creative thoughts to think about having sex.

Make your relationship first. Try having an affair with your husband; call him at work and let him know you want to meet him in the bedroom as soon as he gets home or right after dinner. If you have children, let TV or games babysit for a short time. Reconnect with your husband and have sex before you get tired. Create a rendezvous earlier in the day or evening. Yes, this is going to take some planning and it might not always work, but making your marriage a priority is the key. Don't forget about morning sex, It's a great way to wake up and

immediately puts a smile on your face. You might be su
at how much you enjoy it.

3. What happens when you do not like how your body looks

The first step in the process of feeling confident in your own skin is to read the chapter on self-confidence. There are several exercises and steps mentioned that can help you, but they will take a little time. In the meantime, try implementing a daily exercise routine, as well. This is not about changing your shape, it is about releasing endorphins that will make you feel better about yourself. My friend Lisa Short, a personal trainer and the owner of Body Potential Fitness, says, 'Regular exercise will give you more energy, help you sleep better, release stress, improve your mood, and creates a more positive self-awareness. '

When you are not feeling confident about yourself, changing your look can change your mood. Pretend that you are going on a job interview, kind of.' Put on your most amazing outfit with sexy lingerie underneath, fix your hair and your makeup.

Another change I will challenge you to do is to think about your man's good qualities. Why is he attractive to you? Why do you love him? List his characteristics, favorite body parts, and remember all the good memories from the past. Taking the focus off yourself will help in how you feel.

4. Lack of Libido

Lack of sexual drive can be caused by many things such as imbalanced hormones, illness, medications, and psychological disorders, most of which can be helped by seeing a doctor. If your low sexual desire has been a problem for more than a few months, I suggest you get some help. It may be as simple as talking about it with a professional, or you may need to take a hormone supplement. Creating a daily exercise routine can stimulate feelings of desire, also. However, many women have low sexual drive simply because they are too busy and tired, so try the above suggestions.

5. If you must say NO

Instead of saying no to sex, try rewording it to a 'rain check'. That makes it easier to swallow for men and they know that in the very near future they will get to be with you. Not only does this create some excitement for the future but allows you time to start thinking about it, which will help you get in the mood.

Note: If you agree to a 'rain check' make sure you keep your promise. Not following through with this can be worse than saying no in the first place. Make sure you set a date and time that you both agree on.

6. Just do it!

Think of it like going to the gym on a cold morning. You are tired and it's cold out, but you know if you just get up and go you will feel better. Sex is kind of the same thing. If you are not in the mood let your partner know and maybe together, he can help get you there. Taking extra time to rub and touch, hug and kiss; extended foreplay is the most direct approach to enjoying your time together.

7. Turn off your brain

I have been guilty of this one. I find it very hard to ... and let go during sex if I have things that are not completed. For instance, housework, work deadlines, kid distractions, and so many more. What I started doing a long time ago was to make a list so I wouldn't forget. Think of your mind like a computer screen, if you have too many windows open, your computer runs slow. If you have too many things on your mind, you will be distracted. By making a list you can close the door on most of them because now you will be able to remember what you need to do. Keep a notebook by your bed and take notes as needed.

8. Share a sexual fantasy

Men are usually able to get in the mood a little faster than women. Women need to feel emotionally connected to their man before sexual arousal happens. Try sharing some of your fantasies with a rule that you cannot have sex for at least 20 minutes. Just talking about it will draw you closer, as you talk about the fantasies start touching each other, hugging, kissing, and rubbing your hands all over each other. This sexual attraction will ultimately end the way you both want, perhaps by fulfilling a fantasy.

9. Hold on to each other

Go in for a big bear hug or a make-out kissing session. Holding on to each other for at least 30 seconds has the power to change how you feel. Most people do not get enough physical touch throughout the day. Not only does hugging just feel good but it can change your mood and release stress. There is an actual hormonal change that happens in your body.

While you are in his arms for a hug, nuzzle your nose into his neck and chest and just breathe in his smell. Smell receptors also release endorphins, those happiness hormones. Most women find the smell of their man appealing and sexy as an aphrodisiac.

10. The bedroom

Is your bedroom romantic or does it turn you off because of the mess? Many households use the bedroom as a place to store things away from sight of visitors or kids. Some even use the bed as a place to dump laundry or other things when you get home. This behavior makes going to bed full of additional stress as it needs to be cleaned up or at least moved before you can do anything. By this time any thoughts of sex are out the window. If this sounds a little too familiar take a weekend and clean it up. De-clutter and organize your room so it is clean and relaxing. If funds permit, you should invest in soft sheets and candles. Take some time to decorate and make your room an extension of your sex life.

Let's Face It, Ladies…
What Do Men Want and Need?

*W*hat would a Girlfriend do for a boyfriend in the bedroom? Can you be daring, adventurous and sexy again just like when you first got married?

The Girlfriend does not view sex as a chore or something that they have to do. The Girlfriend looks forward to spending time together and enjoys having sex. She is willing to have fun in the bedroom and looks forward to it. A Girlfriend is prepared with an open mind and a willing, sexy body. Fun, meaningful love-making should be one of the most important parts of your relationship.

Sometimes couples get comfortable in the relationship and life seems to get in the way. Perhaps you are going through troubling times and you just need to break out of a rut. Changing things up in the bedroom can help because sex, intimacy, holding each other close brings you closer together. Even though men tend to be more vocal about how they want and need sex, it is also beneficial for women. You need to be touched, held and cared for just as much as he does. Both men and women desire to experience orgasms as this releases brain chemicals that make you feel emotionally connected to your husband. The Girlfriend Effect is just as much for you to experience love and closeness, as it is for your husband.

The goal is to be The Girlfriend to your Boyfriend. When you share intimate sexual time, it can bring you together and allow love to overcome frustration and hurt. If life in your bedroom has become boring and viewed as a chore, it is time to add some spice and fun. Too many times couples allow small little idiosyncrasies to have an effect on the bedroom atmosphere.

Think of your bedroom as a place where, when you walk thru the door, all other feelings and cares stay on the outside. Do not let the stress of balancing life and family enter into the bedroom. When the little things start to get in the way, that is a good signal that there is something going on with one or both partners and you need to take care of it to prevent it from getting out of control, affecting sexual intimacy, and hurting your relationship.

There may be some people who read this and think, 'How can you always look at the good things and always want to spend time with your guy?' My question back is, 'why not?' I have made it a habit to not look at faults or pet peeves that will cause a problem. I have made a habit to notice the good things and then mention those good things. This allows for greater intimacy. When you enter the bedroom try to have on some 'rose colored glasses' and do not allow attitude, outside sources, or people to influence your actions.

No one is perfect, so why let small things affect your relationship, be forgiving of yourself and of him.

Try stepping outside your comfort zone so that you can experience fun and excitement in the bedroom. Ladies, your men love you and want to spend time with you. Do not hold yourself back sexually because of fear of rejection or embarrassment. I guarantee that your husband thinks you are beautiful and sexy in any way that you are or anything you do. Let that side of you show. If something goes wrong or activities do not go as planned – stay calm and try laughing at yourself.

I know some women are afraid of experimenting in the bedroom because of past experiences or religious beliefs. I encourage you to talk this through as a couple and perhaps you should examine whether certain taboos actually relate to religious beliefs or are just an 'old wives' tale' passed down through generations.

For centuries, sex was thought to only be a reason to procreate. It was not viewed as something couples would use to foster a stronger connection with each other. In the past, sex was not necessarily meant for enjoyment and some still believe this. In my journey living the Girlfriend Effect I have been able to overcome the taboos of sex and intimacy. Walls are being broken down by long standing 'old wives' tales' or taboos such as, sex is sinful or unclean, only men are meant to enjoy sex, you should not touch your body certain ways. Women are becoming more comfortable with their bodies and are not ashamed of being sexy and intimate at every body shape and size. Many women have not had an orgasm because they do not know how or what to do to get there. Often, if an orgasm has been achieved by accident, women do not dare to ask for that again because they were not even sure how it happened. Your body is capable of great pleasure, and you can have an adult discussion with the man you love about what feels good.

Enjoying activities such as masturbation, oral sex, Brazilian waxes, and using sex toys do not make you dirty, they can be a fun and exciting addition to spice things up in the bedroom. Experimentation of these subjects is left for you to discuss with your husband in the privacy of your marriage to determine what works for you both.

Compliment
Accepted

$+$

Compliment

Internalized

$=$

Self-Esteem Boost
Inner Strength

Women are often worried about their bodies and that their husband will judge them, this is simply not true! These are the voices in your own head confirming what you think about yourself. Listen to your husband! Learn to accept a compliment. If your husband states: *'you are beautiful'* or *'you are sexy'* simply say thank you and just enjoy it. Allow your husband to love you and tell you that he loves you the way you are. Whatever you and your partner decide to do to express that love is between the two of you. Sex and intimacy are a vital part of the marriage relationship and has the power to create unbreakable bonds.

When you were first married you were probably willing to make mistakes in the bedroom and then you both had a good laugh. This should still be the case. For instance; if one of you rolls off the bed during sexual play; can you laugh about it? Of course! Laughing together creates bonds of love that strengthen your relationship.

Laughing, good feelings, and friendship are all necessary components of a strong relationship. There are actually chemicals released in your brain when you laugh, feel good, and have fun. When people say *laughter is the best medicine*, it's true! The brain produces endorphins, the same hormones as when you have sex. Laughter and fun get your blood flowing and send more oxygen to your brain, relieving stress and possibly even healing a heart wounded from discord. So have fun and laugh with each other as you live the Girlfriend Effect.

If your husband is self-conscious with his body or sexual confidence (yes, men have self-esteem issues, too) you need to give him honest compliments and praise both in life and the bedroom. Give him encouragement especially in the bedroom so that he will want to try new things. Keep your conversations light and have fun. For example, tell him what you like, tell him he is sexy, grab his butt, you might be surprised to find out what he likes. Putting in effort is better than being perfect in the bedroom. Make your bedroom a safe space, a place of romance and intimacy.

JODI HARMAN

Benefits of Sex

*H*ow can you have a real, exciting, fun and fulfilling sexual relationship if you do not talk about it, explore each other and share how you feel about sex?

Living the Girlfriend Effect is about being willing to be closer and more intimate, to be the best friend and lover you can be. Whether you are a couple having sex more often or (heaven forbid) less often, I am going to encourage you to start with at least a minimum of twice a week, if you are already at twice a week, add two more days. The goal is to have sex more often which will help your relationship and you will both be happier.

In addition to the emotional benefits, sex can improve your immune system, heart health, mental stimulation, and sleep while burning calories and decreasing stress (Robinson, 2013). Sex makes you happy and the lack thereof makes you unhappy. That is why there are so many unhappy people; they aren't getting enough attention and sex.

In one of my favorite books, *Think and Grow Rich, Napoleon Hill* has this to say about sexual desires:

'Sexual desire is the most powerful of human desires. When driven by this desire, men develop keenness of imagination, courage, will-power, persistence, and creative ability unknown to them at other times. So strong and impelling is the desire for sexual contact that men freely run the risk of life and reputation to indulge it.' (Hill, 1937)

Although this quote is directed at men and may be old, it still rings true for modern men and women.

Too many couples do not talk about what they want from sex. However, if you start to talk about another subject they definitely know what they like and do not like. For instance, if you were preparing to go out on a date and your husband really loves steak and you really want pasta but the restaurants that you each want to go to does not serve what the other wants, what are you going to do to solve the problem? Compromise and choose a place that has more variety.

Couples usually talk about what they want in all other areas of life, but not the bedroom. I think that there may be some apprehension in talking about sex because we have so few healthy examples available. Parents usually do not talk about their sex lives with their children, even if it was a happy and healthy one. It is a particularly taboo subject for many who grew up in strict religious household.

But remember you are married now and it is okay to have sex AND talk about sex with your husband. Living the Girlfriend Effect will allow you to explore options and be adventurous as you explore each other's bodies to find out what each person likes and doesn't like. Take this opportunity to let your husband know how much you love him and allow him to show you love in return. Sex is a natural part of marriage and is the most beautiful form of showing someone that you truly love and care for them.

Too many couples allow intimacy to become the lowest priority in their lives. They wait until they are spent from the challenges of the day to attempt to have a sexual experience. When one partner needs and desires sex often and the other wants it less often, it can leave the couple with feelings of rejection, hurt, sadness and despair.

An idea I would like to share with you may seem impossible to some people and for others may seem easy and exciting. I suggest that you set an expectation of having sex every day, even book time on the calendar if that is what it takes. There may be times when sex just isn't going to work and if not, it is okay. But do not let the habit of going several days without sex build again. Do not put your relationship last!

If you are struggling with finding ideas, check out the chapter on flirting and fantasies.

Men Love It When You...

C ouples often have the misconception that sex just happens but that is just not true. Each person needs time to prepare for sex.

Women are great at multi-tasking and often have a million things running through their minds. This can interfere with a woman's ability to get aroused. You need to take the time to quiet the distractions in your brain, let your body relax and get tuned into your husband for sex. Usually, guys are able to move on their sexual feelings faster than women. But they still need foreplay to improve the overall experience.

The foreplay gets the emotions and hormones headed in the direction of sexual arousal. This is where it becomes imperative to do all the things in this book. By keeping your partner, and the idea of having sex with him, in your mind throughout the day, your body is primed and better prepared to enjoy touches and intimacy once you are together.

Think about the last time you went camping, once you build the fire you have to pay attention or it will go out. You turn the coals, put on more kindling and keep the fire smoldering. Foreplay is like the fire in that you pay attention all the time, give your husband a little look, rub against each other, or even have a quick or long make-out session. This will make the desire for sex later in the day much more intense.

I want you
In the worst
way

Men love to be touched, caressed and rubbed. Take time to sit by each other, hold hands, brush up against his body. Rubbing your hands all over his body says, 'I want you.' Try using different pressures of touch and your fingernails for different sensations that he will enjoy. If you are able, pin him up against the door and kiss him sensually while starting to take off his clothes as he walks in the door from work. After about 15 minutes of this stop and have dinner together. By building his arousal then backing off, you are increasing his desire for you.

As the evening progresses, he will not be able to take his hands off you. Try kissing and rubbing up against each other all over the house and bedroom. The different surfaces, heights, and positions will bring an awareness of what you might be missing by staying in the bed to have sex.

1. Sofa loveseat or lounger (might remind you of dating) – allows for different heights and supports the body while trying different positions.
2. Chairs; kitchen, office, arm chair, big and bulky chair, bar stool– allows for differing heights, body positions, possible for both to be able to have movement and full body contact. A lap dance is the perfect way to get in the mood for sex, especially if he gets naked too.
3. Standing or leaning up against a wall – supports different heights and can help you achieve full body contact.
4. Do nothing but kiss each other above the waist; on the lips, ears, neck, nipples, shoulders, etc. for double the amount time you would normally engage in foreplay.

5. One night, agree to try each other's favorite positions for sex constantly changing all through the experience.

6. Have sex outside (in your yard, at night) and leave your clothes far away from where you will be. For some reason this seems naughty and illegal which heightens the arousal.

7. Leave the lingerie and stiletto heels on while you have sex. The height difference makes it more interesting. You will also have a heightened awareness from trying to keep your balance that will leave you and him feeling fulfilled.

8. While he's showering, ambush him without saying a word. Use squeezable food like whip cream, jello, or chocolate and get dirty together, then wash each other off.

9. Try to take off all his clothes...using only your mouth. Then beg him to help you take off his pants.

10. Surprise him with blindfolds for both of you. You will have to feel your way around each other, especially during foreplay.

11. Make sure to get ready for your time together. You will feel better about yourself and be a little more daring if you have freshened up. For instance, take a shower, if you have time, and apply a scented and sparkly lotion (his favorite smell or yours). Wear your favorite color, or better yet, wear red. Red attracts your man's attention. Choose red lingerie and a sexy red dress with high heels. You will feel like a million bucks.

12. Give your hubby a sensual massage (I recommend getting a massage table) Get your favorite sensual smell and some coconut oil or other oil and just rub his entire body. Not only will this help you get in the mood, but he will be all relaxed before you get him excited again. The physical touch allows you both to focus on each other, fulfills that desire for

closeness, and allows you to just be in the moment with each other.

13. If your bedroom is feeling dull and uninviting, take some time to romanticize it up. Get some candles, rearrange the furniture, get new sheets or just spray the sheets you have with a romantic smell that you both like.

14. Take a bath together. Use the time to touch, relax and caress each other. Just see where it leads you.

15. Sexting is texting with pictures; suggestive pictures. If you are not sure what to send, start with a close up of your lips: kissing lips, licking lips, or a sexy smile will get his attention. As you get comfortable, you can show a little cleavage or arrange his favorite lingerie on the bed – use your imagination and send him images that will turn him on. This should keep you both thinking about each other all day. Don't be surprised if you get a picture back in return. (Reminder – many phones will show a small thumbnail of an image that is sent via text. If your hubby is at work or has his phone out in public, others may see what you sent. For more privacy: I like to start with a text that says; 'The next one is for you! Are you ready?' Then wait for his reply before I send.)

16. Touch as much as possible. The body releases pleasure hormones when a person is touched, it is the glue that bonds you together.

17. Men are usually competitive and if you are too, then why not bring on your full game attitude. Friendly competition can actually cause a chemical reaction in the body, as well as, getting you both turned on at the same time. Make sure to keep

things light hearted and fun. Go bowling, play basketball, soccer, tennis; just have fun.

18. Additionally, both men and women get turned on by reading or watching a romantic movie (you choose your comfort level). This can help you be creative with ideas and get your mind thinking about each other.

There is another chapter on flirting, so this is a reminder to really turn it on. Mastering the art of flirting keeps the love alive. The expectation of having sex every day is the key to flirting all the time. Women do this to keep their man sexually charged! Plus, admit it ladies, We just really love the attention we get when our man notices us. You need to do things that keep him interested in wanting to be with you, and to miss you when you are not together.

The foreplay is the most important part of all the fantasy excitement because you need to put a little thought into planning. This allows for you to start the foreplay well before the time you set. Remember when you were a little kid and your birthday was coming up? You looked forward to it for several weeks and as the time drew closer, so did the excitement.

Foreplay is about building the excitement and sexual tension that makes you think about each other all day, every day. Get creative about how to build the excitement between you before you can even touch. Then, extend that time of just touching to make 'the main event' that much more exciting and fulfilling for both of you.

Why Men Love Lingerie

*L*ingerie opens the door for women to change their frame of mind and get into the Girlfriend role leaving the other roles of career women, mother, housewife tucked away for another time.

Every woman wants to be viewed as beautiful, wanted, and sexy. Lingerie plays a crucial role in the sensual and sexy part of a relationship (even if it cannot be seen on the outside). Wearing lingerie will make you feel better about how you look and improves self-esteem. Sexy underclothing also creates a flirty or naughty aspect to the outfit, which heightens the senses and transmits foreplay signals to your man. When you feel good about your body, you exude self-confidence, which is very sexy. This little secret that no one (except your husband) has to know can make a huge difference in how you show up for everything in life.

Even if you start wearing sexy lingerie everyday, that feeling does not go away.

Both men and women should participate in the purchasing of lingerie, both buy for similar reasons. Men buy lingerie for their wives partially for selfish reasons, but also for the changes he sees in his wife when she has it on. Remember, men love to see their wife wear sexy clothes and do not see all the flaws and imperfections that the wife usually is looking at.

When shopping for any clothes make sure to add lingerie to your must-have list and always have a few surprises to ignite some passion as you live the Girlfriend Effect. Your husband will always appreciate it when you wear lingerie.

Some pieces are meant to be removed quickly, while others can be comfortably worn all day. As your budget allows, add pieces that make you feel beautiful. Many women complain of the lace being itchy or the confining fit of lingerie. As you shop, take the time to find high quality pieces that are comfortable and fit properly so you can wear it all day. Pulling body parts back into place all day is not a sexy look and comfort is important, otherwise the underwear will distract from the sensual feelings you are trying to create.

Make sure to wear a variety of different types of pieces that enhance your body. If you choose to wear simple lingerie, your man may know that you feel the need to relax and be taken care of. If you go full out with kinky and fantasy lingerie, he will also know what you have on your mind. This is the perfect time to bring some fantasy play into the relationship. Keep him guessing and yearning for more.

Men like a variety of lingerie pieces, so here are some basic ideas that are sure to please. All of these look great while wearing very high heels. Men love a woman in heels because it accentuates their legs and other curves. Women also have better posture when wearing heels, so wear them as much as possible (if you can).

Babydoll

The Babydoll looks like a bra with a short skirt attached to the band that barely (or doesn't quite) cover the butt. They enhance the curves of any women by focusing attention on men's favorite body parts. It leaves just enough skin showing that it turns him on. Usually, these come with sexy bikini or thong underwear.

Chemise

A flowy silk-like mini-dress leaves him guessing what is underneath. Add some sexy panties for some spice. All men love a sexy pair of panties.

Camisole & Thong

I am not talking about wearing something old and raggedy. Choose one that is soft and clings to your curves, then pair it with a thong or some lacy panties. This is a simple, sexy look. Put in a little effort with some lipstick and fix your hair. Since you probably already own these pieces, this is a great choice if you are not in a position to invest in lingerie right now.

Teddy

A very, very sexy piece with secret openings for pleasure. Men enjoy the journey of finding their way around your sexy body.

Push-Up Bra, G-string, Garter Belts, Stockings & High Heels

I think men everywhere would be sad if this one was not on the list, as most have a fantasy or two about this outfit. This is not going to change anytime soon. It has been seducing men for years so you should really know how to rock the garter belts stockings and high heels. The sexiest colors to wear are black and red. Flaunting hints of what is under your clothes will have your man wondering when the entire outfit will be revealed and leave him wanting you more.

Because lingerie is usually reserved for a special occasion, it can make your man feel loved and that you really want to please him, especially if you wear something he picked out for you. Give him a little peek when he gets home from work, or better yet, send him a text at lunch time to let him know what you have planned for him.

This extended foreplay can be intense as you flaunt your sexiness around the house, during dinner or even while doing the dishes. The anticipation of getting you alone and revealing what is underneath is a real turn on. Allow this to lead into a full-blown, sensual kissing fest as it all comes off. Give him a private show, then enjoy what happens once everything comes off.

Log onto our website for all sizes of sexy, fun lingerie from some of our favorite designers, www.GirlfriendEffect.com.

Sexual Adventures and Fantasies

F antasies are all about being daring and exciting, trying new things that stretch the relationship and bring fun and pleasure back.

Remember the feelings from the first time you made love? Remember how nervous and scared and excited you were all at the same time. Acting out fantasies can bring those feelings back.

Both partners should always be prepared and ready to have sex. Sex is another form of enjoyment and pleasure, it should not be viewed as another responsibility or only for making babies.

Sex is way for a couple to connect and show how you really feel about each other. Too many women think that men just want to have sex for their own pleasure. But, if both partners are putting the relationship first, these feelings will dissipate, and love will enter back in. So, have fun exploring different rooms in the house, different surfaces, or go outside. Be willing to find new places to have sex. Be daring. If you are worried about privacy (it can actually be exciting) then do a little planning and start with a tent or blanket to cover up. You never know where you will end up.

Fantasy and role-playing scenarios give each of you the opportunity to be someone else in or out of the bedroom. It lets you step out of your normal role and comfort zone. Role-playing allows both partners to share fantasies. Your relationship needs to be a safe place for you to be open and share with each other without judgment or denial. Whether you are just starting out with role-playing or have been doing it for some time, remember that the most important part is open, honest communication with your partner. Be respectful of each other's likes and dislikes and set boundaries that you both agree upon. Some fantasies may require one or both of you to get outside your comfort zone, or even out of the house. With open communication you can decide together how far you want to take each fantasy.

When we were kids, we all enjoyed playing dress up. That's because we were able to use our imaginations and we could be anybody we wanted. We could go anywhere and experience amazing things. We could have different accents, a different personality. We could be the boss or the hero/heroine. So, why have we given up this part of life? As adults we need to be creative and use our imaginations. We can be more adventurous now than we could back then. You can explore the limitless world of sexual fantasy. You are able to explore different sides of yourself and your partner. Role-playing will spark your creativity and reignite the passion within your relationship. The amazing fun and excitement it will bring to your relationships will astound you.

Don't start with a complicated role-play, take it slow and easy. You need to become accustomed to this new part of your relationship. It may seem awkward and you may be embarrassed at first, but it doesn't matter. It is your fantasy and no one else will know. As you both get more comfortable role-playing, your fantasies will feed your imagination and your intimate relationship will skyrocket upward.

Once you decide you want to role-play in your intimate relationship there are a couple of components that are important to make your experience amazing. First, you each need to get into character for the role play. This is an opportunity to act different and move out of that safe, mundane role we all have with our partners. Think of those hot movie or TV scenes you like to watch. Be that actor or actress and try some of those moves, imitate how they talk, act the way they act. You are that Call Girl or that Boss, so act like it. Embody that character. Don't do anything you normally would. Explore all those hidden sexual desires you want to try.

Next, you need to stage the scene to provide the atmosphere and the mood for the role play. You don't want to always act out the role in your bedroom. Transform your bedroom to the scene you are playing: a doctor's office, professional office, or classroom. As you both become more comfortable, you can move your role playing out of the house to your dates using different venues for your scenes.

The last thing is you each need to do is dress the part you are portraying. You can find erotic lingerie costumes for some scenarios and regular costumes for others. The costumes help you portray that character for the evening. Acting out scenarios and dynamics that are different from your everyday life experience is a major reason role-playing scenar incredibly arousing.

There are some things you don't want to do during your role-playing: You should never disrespect, humiliate, or abuse your partner. Leave any cruelty out of your role-playing so that your memories of these amazing experiences are just that, amazing. No one is expecting an Oscar winning performance so be patient with yourself and your hubby.

Your role-playing can be as simple or elaborate as you want it to be. Then, get into your roles and let the fun begin. I have collected a list of affiliates on the website to help with costumes and lingerie: www.GirlFriendEffect.com. Whether you purchase something new or put together a costume from what's already in your closet, the important thing to remember is to have fun with your husband.

If this is your first time with fantasies, try just to keep it light and fun: Go back to where you met for the first time and recreate the whole thing over again. Just pretend, act like boyfriend and girlfriend. Go see a movie and make-out through the entire movie until your lips hurt. Have dinner and talk the whole time trying to find what each person likes and doesn't like.

Another idea to ignite your relationship, try 'parking' just like you did when you were dating. Find a deserted road or parking lot and have fun making out in the car. This is still fun even though you are married. The excitement of possibly getting discovered by the police is still there. Try it. Too many people think because you are married you should not be doing stuff like this, my response is, 'Why not?'

In role-play you can stay in character for the whole evening or just to get things going. Most people find a place in-between that is comfortable for them. A big part of role-play is getting into character, or the headspace of actually being that person. In doing that you need to dress the part. It doesn't have to be a fancy costume if you don't want. Some sexy lingerie, jewelry or those high heels may be all that's needed. It could even be the right makeup or maybe a mask to help slip into character. Remember, it is all about the fun so don't be afraid to get out of your comfort zone and wear something that you may not usually wear.

In role-play you need to plan out each scene you are doing beforehand. Often this planning session is great foreplay to the actual scene. It can be just as intimate and erotic as the scene itself. Once you have had your play session, take time to review it and see what worked or didn't work for each of you. You don't need have an in-depth review like a work project, but talking about it will help make the next role-play scene even better.

Role-playing with your partner is a way to build on your relationship together. You improve communication skills, build trust in each other and truly accept your partner. This is a great opportunity to add fun to your relationship journey. Plan to play naughty!

I have listed a few role playing scenarios and how you can act them out in your intimate relationship.

Naughty Nurse Scenario

Characters: A naughty nurse and the strikingly handsome new doctor.

Stage/scene: The scene may be set up in two different locations. First, would be setting your bedroom like a hospital room. Remove clutter so it is a basic looking room. Alternate scene would be to set up your living room/family room like a hospital staff break room.

Wardrobe: Sexy nurse's costume (not scrubs), doctor's lab coat. Add any accessories you would like, such as a stethoscope, clipboard, or other medical items.

Action: A new doctor has started working at your hospital on the night shift. You want to be selected for part of his staff so you try to seduce him either in a vacant hospital room or in the staff break room.

Night Club Pick-Up Scenario

Characters: A hot, sexy chick out for a fun night and an attractive businessman in town for the weekend.

Stage/scene: You will be going to a local night club, lounge, or bar. Either reserve a room at a local hotel or make up your bedroom like a hotel room. (You will need a baby sitter for this one because you may not make it home until really late.)

Wardrobe: High skirt, high heels and low cut top. Business attire with loose tie. (You may need the tie later!!)

Action: Both of you need to arrive at the club separately. You are strangers to each other. You are out for a night of fun at the local club and he is in town for the week on business. He is out for some fun and maybe a fling. He sees you on the dance floor or across from him at the bar and buys you a drink and sends it over. You catch his eye with a flirty sensual look. He asks you to dance and you sit together and talk. Next thing you know you agree to accompany him to his car for a sensual make-out session and then head back to his hotel for some hot, heavy sex. It's only for tonight so anything goes.

High-Class Call Girl Scenario

Characters: A call girl dressed to turn him on and a powerful business executive.

Stage/scene: Your bedroom set up either like a hotel room that he is staying in or a naughty boudoir room she uses for her clients. Silky sheets, candles, no clutter or personal items around. Alternatively, you can reserve a hotel room.

Wardrobe: Sexy cocktail dress with a high slit and low cut neckline, high heels, stockings, sexy lingerie, big sexy hair, and red lipstick. Business suit and briefcase.

Action: He has requested your services for the night. You are there to fulfill all of your client's desires. You will be paid well for your services and if you are extraordinary in your job, there will be a large tip. If you have a hotel room, you can meet in the hotel bar for dinner and drinks before heading to "his" room.

Lingerie Model and Fashion Show Scenario

Characters: Model walking runway at fashion show and a top modeling agent.

Stage/scene: Set your bedroom or living room up as a fashion show stage. Have an area laid out as a runway. Have several chairs set up for guests to sit on. Need to have refreshments and drinks for guests. Have a backstage area where you change and have all of your lingerie outfits laid out in order you are going to be wearing them in.

Wardrobe: Have 6-12 outfits to model that include high heels, stockings, garter belts, panties, bras, teddies, babydolls, chemises. He should be in casual business attire or a nice suit.

Action: He is a top modeling agent and has come to this fashion show specifically to view you and offer you a contract with his agency. You need to impress him and show off your 'assets'. Maybe a little one on one time will seal the deal. You could always invite him back to the dressing area and seduce him.

Stripper at a Men's Club Scenario

Character: An exotic dancer and a VIP customer.

Stage/scene: Set your bedroom or living room up to resemble a gentlemen's club. A stripper pole would be great. You need to have a dining/kitchen chair to also use plus any other props you can think of like a feather boa or long gloves. Need to have some sexy, sensual music you can dance and gyrate too. Take some time to select your music. Have $30-$40 one dollar bills or some play money for him to use.

Wardrobe: High heels, stockings, sexy lingerie or dance/club wear. He can be in casual wear.

Action: A VIP customer has requested a private audience with you. You escort him to the private viewing room and give him a show and lap dance. Remember this is a private viewing so there are no rules or limits. Anything goes, so touching is encouraged and expected. For a little bit more, you get naked along with your customer and give him another lap dance. Who knows what will happen now!

Cougar on the Prowl Scenario

Characters: A hot cougar looking for a young stud and a young waiter at restaurant.

Stage/scene: Set up your kitchen like a restaurant and/or bar area, complete with snacks and cocktails or wine.

Wardrobe: Hot dress and heels with sexy lingerie. He can wear dark slacks, white shirt and a short apron.

Action: You are a hot cougar out for dinner with your girlfriends. Unfortunately, they have had to cancel, so you continue on with your dinner plans alone. You notice your waiter is the type of stud you are looking for. You flirt with him through dinner and he stays past his shift to finish his service with you. He joins you for a drink and you invite him back to your place. He is excited and willing to go. Back in your bedroom you take charge and teach him how to please and satisfy a woman. When you are done with him you send him on his way.

Sexy Secretary and Horny Boss Scenario

Characters: A sexy, naughty secretary and a boss that flirts all the time.

Stage/scene: Set your bedroom, living room or kitchen up to resemble an office. A desk, chair and couch are needed. If you have access to an actual office, try that setting.

Wardrobe: Short skirt/dress and low cut blouse or button up blouse, and high heels. He should be in a business suit.

Action: It is getting close to the end of the work day and your boss asks if you could stay late to help with a project that is due for presentation in the morning. You quickly agree because you have been trying for months to seduce your boss. He is always flirting with you and you want to take it all the way. As everyone else leaves the building you work with him inside his private office. You turn up the heat with your flirting, your blouse is unbuttoned further than normal and your skirt is riding up your thigh. You bend over to pick up some files and give him a glimpse of your panties. You lean over often to give him a good look at your cleavage. Your evil plan has worked and you complete your seduction.

Sexy Business Woman Scenario

Characters: Executive business woman who likes to tease her male employee by wearing sexy clothing and making suggestive comments and the employee who enjoys the attention of his female boss.

Stage/scene: Set your bedroom, living room or kitchen up to resemble an office. A desk, chair and couch are needed. If you have access to an actual office, try that setting.

Wardrobe: Short skirt/dress and low cut blouse or button up blouse, and high heels. He should be in a business suit.

Action: It is lunch time and all of the employees have left the office, except for one and he is your favorite. You ask him into your office to help with some filing you need done. Little does he know that the only work you need done in your office

.ight now is for him to satisfy your burning sexual needs. Your blouse is unbuttoned real low and your skirt is high on your thighs. What and where is up to you.

Fitness Trainer and Trainee Scenario

Character: Yoga Instructor and a new yoga student.

Stage/ Scene: Set your bedroom, living room to resemble a yoga studio or gym. You will need yoga mats or towels. If you know enough yoga to make this work that's fine otherwise, borrow or buy a yoga video.

Wardrobe: Start out with just sexy underwear - you will end wearing nothing.

Actions: He has requested your services to learn how to do yoga. You are there to teach (fulfill all of your client's desires). He needs help stretching and getting into the poses. Clothes become irrelevant and you both loose them quickly. Try yoga poses together.

Remember to have fun and do not try to judge yourself or husband about things that go wrong when trying to create scenarios or fun fantasies. Things might not always go as planned and that is okay. Remember, Hollywood has someone that cuts out all the goof ups. Life is real, so enjoy and remember to laugh at yourselves!

If you would like more Fantasy ideas visit our website GirlfriendEffect.com.

(Disclaimer: Reader takes full responsibilities for their actions when attempting any ideas or concepts in this book. The Author will not be held liable for reader's actions.)

JODI HARMAN

Live the Girlfriend Experience

What Girlfriends Do

*W*hen you fully embrace the Girlfriend Effect, your marriage gets stronger, more loving, and you are both happier. A girlfriend always makes sure to:

1. If a day goes by without touching your man, your desire to be with him becomes very strong and you start to think about ways to see him, touch him, and be intimate as soon as possible.

2. Your drawers are overflowing with sexy lingerie, and you are not afraid to wear it any time of day or night. Just for fun, you wear it under your clothes to help you get in the mood a little more. Hint: If you give your hubby a flash of what you wearing (or not wearing) you both get turned-on more.

3. When scheduling out your day/week you make sure to schedule spending time together and having sex is a priority, even if it means that other parts of life do not get completed. (Who cares if the dishes are not done?)

4. You are adventurous and willing to try new things in the bedroom and outside of the bedroom. You are willing to have sex anywhere, anytime, or on anything. (Ideas: The floor, dining room table, desk, shower, beach, car, etc.)

5. If you are busy with work or housework, dishes, or making the bed and your hubby interrupts to talk or have sex, you are willing. You look forward to spending time with him. You make it a priority to stop what you are doing and give him a hug, a sensual kiss, or run away somewhere private in the house just to have sex. (If possible, put a movie on for the kids, and make sure you lock the door.)

6. You know your body and are not afraid to let your man know what you like and do not like when it comes to being loved, kissed, touched and during sex. Being desired by him makes you feel powerful and sexy.

7. You are not afraid to share your date and sex fantasies. As your hubby shares his fantasies, you are ready and willing to play them out. Honestly, you will try anything once, especially role-playing and sex games, to ignite intimacy constantly. (Hint: If you own a pair of handcuffs, don't be afraid to use them.)

8. You make sure you and your husband are always satisfied both emotionally and physically. You love being touched literally anywhere on your body and soak in the love and attention.

9. Losing some sleep in exchange for spending time together and/or having sex is never a problem. (Hints: Try taking a nap so you aren't too tired. Instead of pajamas wear lingerie to bed, or nothing at all. Show up ready to have sex.)

10. Reading this makes you want to spend time with your hubby right now and find somewhere to run away and have sex as soon as possible.

Girlfriend Challenge

*I*n a stable marriage with normal ups and downs, there will always be room for growth.

So many issues in marriage can be summarized by these few words: self-esteem, confidence, empathy, open communication, love, and kindness. These are not hard things to do but it does take conscious effort and a little time. Don't you think your marriage is worth it?

I hope that you found the tips, techniques, and teachings you need to make your marriage a priority and find the love that has been missing since life became too busy. No two marriages are the same, as each person in each marriage has their likes and dislikes, their own personalities. That means that everything in this book may not be right for you, but you don't know what works until you try the techniques for yourself.

Be intentional in your actions and reactions to your husband. There is a myth out in the world that fighting and quarreling with one another is just a normal part of being married, but that is simply not true. From time to time there will be disappointments and possibly arguments but don't let

Lucado says it best, 'Conflict is
'onal.'

and love with your full heart

husband wants or is thinking.
will find out. I challenge you to honestly
and:

'How can I be a better wife?'
'What can I do to help you?'
'What can I do to make you feel loved?'

When he answers these questions, you will know what you need to do. Make sure you listen closely. I recommend asking these questions often as situations and feelings can change.

You may not even have to do anything more than to ask these questions, but if you ever need to spice things up, keep this book handy.

I am sure that you have some unmet goal or expectation in your life because you were too scared of what others might say, possibly of what you might say to yourself. I know I have, this book for instance has taken me years to finally write and send out to the world. All too often we let fear, trepidation, or insecurities override all our good ideas and intentions.

How many of you have wanted to try something new only to be stopped by what is going on in your own head? These feelings are natural, but how do we overcome them? How do we take all those thoughts and ideas we have for our life and especially our relationship and bring them to fruition?

Let's look at how to do this as a Girlfriend to your husband. A recurring theme throughout this book and in working to improve our relationship in general is open, honest communication with our spouse.

As a couple you must create a safe space (physical and mental) within your relationship where you are free from criticism and judgment. You or your partner may be shy and timid about opening up, but you should not stress about it. Your relationship should be a safe space where you can play, have fun, laugh and enjoy new experiences together. Remember, it should never be embarrassing to share your intimate desires with your husband. After all, that's what a relationship is all about, sharing your lives together.

Within this space you will be able to experience amazing new things together because you are both in harmony. Yes, this will be a little uncomfortable at first. But it is only by moving outside our comfort zone that we truly grow. As in every aspect of your life, your marriage relationship should always be constantly growing and learning. Pushing ourselves and each other outside that familiar zone of comfort. Besides, the thrill of new adventures can be fun and addicting, so experience it with someone you love.

If this sounds familiar and you want to upgrade your relationship with your husband, use the Girlfriend Effect. I challenge you to be comfortable with being uncomfortable by trying new things, new adventures. Take some time to figure out what it is that you really want from your relationship in all areas: communication, support, love, intimacy, and sex. Then, find out what your husband's wants, needs and desires are. Do a little research on your ideas, or do it together for more fun. Be prepared to elaborate and share fully with your spouse.

The Girlfriend Effect is designed to give your husband the Girlfriend experience by creating more intimacy, passion, and love in your relationship. It's not about changing you into something you're not, rather that you expand your knowledge and expertise about yourself, your husband, sex, communication, and your relationship.

Enjoy,
Jodi Harman

References

Hill, N. (1937). Think and Grow Rich. In N. Hill, Think and Grow Rich (Chapter 11).

Merriam Webster Dictionary. (2016, January 16). *Merriam Webster Dictionary. Retrieved from Merriam Webster Dictionary : http://www.merriam-webster.com/dictionary/self c...*

Moberg, K. U. (2003). *The Oxytocin Factor: Taping the hormone of calm, love and healing. In K. U. Moberg, The Oxytocin Factor: Taping the hormone of calm, love and healing. Da Capo Press. Retrieved June 2015, from https://books.google.com/books?id=Ehed6dPMqakC&pri...*

Robinson, K. M. (2013, October 24). *10 Surprising Health Benefits of Sex. Retrieved January 2016, from WebMD: http://www.webmd.com/sex-relationships/guide/sex-a...*

US Bureau of Labor Statistics. (2014). *American Time Use Survey. Retrieved September 2015, from US Departemtn Labor and Stistics: http://www.bls.gov/tus/charts/*

Images by Dreamstime.com © and DepositPhoto.com

JODI HARMAN

Special Thanks To

*M*y husband and love of my life, Mark Harman. He is truly that greatest man I know. Without his love, friendship, patience, and encouragement I would be lost. He helped me to write and research some of the chapters so I would be able to share ideas and desires from a man's perspective.

My children for all their love and patience with me as a mother, and now as fans and supporters of me.

Spencer Harman and Family

Camilla & Jacob Rapp and Family

Grant & Kersty Harman and Family

Colin & Elizabeth Harman and Family

The mentors who have inspired and empowered me to grow, especially through rough times in my life:

Joel Bauer, A true Mentor that gives from the heart, answers all my questions and inspires me to dig deeper and give from the heart.

www.joelbauer.com

Jack Canfield, a master at working through problems to find answers and success. www.jackcanfield.com

Tiffany Peterson, a caring mentor and friend that inspired me to be better than I was and changed my mindset from *lacking* to *I am enough*. She taught me to love myself. www.TiffanySpeaks.com

Ann Webb, a dear friend that touches lives around the world with her life's work. Her program of Ideal Life Vision has increased my chance of happiness and success www.theannwebb.com

Christi Diamond, who facilitates healing from the inside out. www.thehealingcoach.com

Adryenn Ashley for her creativity and fun attitude. www.wowisme.net

About the Author

*J*odi's life is dedicated to helping women and men... Reconnect, Recommit, and Reignite their deep passion for each other by inspiring women to live the Girlfriend Effect.

Jodi touches lives all over the world with her live conferences, intimate seminars, and relationship building retreats. Couples find that they are reunited, recommitted, and passionate about making their relationship more than they ever thought possible.

Jodi resides in California with her husband, Mark and their family. She enjoys traveling and making new memories with family and friends. Jodi is a mother of four children and at the time of this publishing six grandchildren that she loves to teach, learn and play with.

For free courses, marriage help and to connect with Jodi
www.jodiharman.com

Made in the USA
Columbia, SC
25 January 2018